Crisis and Pandemic Leadership

ABOUT THE COVER

The cover illustration, beautifully designed by one of our contributors, Kristen M. Snyder, represents new growth that emerges from responsive leadership during a crisis. The base of the photo represents the sense of chaos and lack of clarity that characterize crises. As leaders gather amid the chaos, building strength through collaboration, new growth emerges through the roots of the tree that are responsive, resilient, and sustainable, no matter the crisis. The photo image in the center of the design is of the four leaders at Corbett Preparatory School of IDS in Tampa, Florida, who together reflect diversity through background, experience, age, race, and gender. Nicholas Rodriquez is a Hispanic male, serving his first year as headmaster of the school. Dr. Joyce B. Swarzman is a female of Jewish decent, who served as the school's headmaster over twenty-seven years and now has assumed a new leadership role in the school. Michael Johnson is a Scottish-born male who is currently in his third year as associate headmaster. Jenn Jagdmann has been the middle school division leader for five years. Together, this team continues to build on the school's strong foundation with the laws of science that are presented in chapter one. Their success today has emerged from the now deeply rooted traditions of collaboration, cooperative learning, teaming, networking, and working as a strong complex adaptive system to become "One Community."

Crisis and Pandemic Leadership

Implications for Meeting the Needs of Students, Teachers, and Parents

Edited by Jeffrey Glanz

ROWMAN & LITTLEFIELD
Lanham • Boulder • New York • London

Published by Rowman & Littlefield
An imprint of The Rowman & Littlefield Publishing Group, Inc.
4501 Forbes Boulevard, Suite 200, Lanham, Maryland 20706
www.rowman.com

6 Tinworth Street, London SE11 5AL, United Kingdom

Copyright © 2021 by Jeffrey Glanz

All rights reserved. No part of this book may be reproduced in any form or by any electronic or mechanical means, including information storage and retrieval systems, without written permission from the publisher, except by a reviewer who may quote passages in a review.

British Library Cataloguing in Publication Information Available

Library of Congress Cataloging-in-Publication Data

Names: Glanz, Jeffrey, editor.
Title: Crisis and pandemic leadership : implications for meeting the needs of students, teachers, and parents / edited by Jeffrey Glanz.
Description: Lanham, Maryland : Rowman & Littlefield, 2021. | Series: School leadership series | Includes bibliographical references and index. | Summary: "This book provides the theoretical and practical strategies necessary for a school leader to confront the many crises that inevitably occur"— Provided by publisher.
Identifiers: LCCN 2021006297 (print) | LCCN 2021006298 (ebook) | ISBN 9781475860627 (cloth) | ISBN 9781475860634 (paperback) | ISBN 9781475860641 (epub)
Subjects: LCSH: Educational leadership. | School management and organization. | Crisis management. | Social distancing (Public health) and education. | COVID-19 Pandemic, 2020-
Classification: LCC LB2806 .C694 2021 (print) | LCC LB2806 (ebook) | DDC 371.2—dc23
LC record available at https://lccn.loc.gov/2021006297
LC ebook record available at https://lccn.loc.gov/2021006298

Contents

Series Editor's Introduction		1
Editor's Introduction		5
1	Building Sustainable Systems of Schooling in Turbulent Times: Big Ideas from the Sciences *Karolyn J. Snyder and Kristen M. Snyder*	7
2	Educating in and Beyond a Crisis: An Australian Perspective *Lisa Vinnicombe*	23
3	The Challenge of Inequity in Educational Systems Under the Coronavirus Pandemic and Other Crises: Toward a New Model of Teacher Mentoring *Orly Shapira-Lishchinsky*	35
4	A Swerve in Practice in Times of Crises: Rethinking Teacher Evaluation Anew *Helen M. Hazi*	47
5	Rethinking Character Education in the Era of Online Schooling in Crises *Shazia Rehman Khan*	59
6	Instructional Leadership in Times of Crises and the Goal of Schooling *Haim Shaked*	71

7 Crisis Leadership: Principals' Resilience Under Extraordinary Pressure *Mary Lynne Derrington and Sonya Hayes*	83
8 Changing Educational Paradigms through Distance Learning: Challenges and Opportunities During and After School Crises *Shmuel Shenhav and Ayal Geffon*	101
9 The Impact of School Crises on Students and Families from a Social-Justice Perspective: Practical Suggestions for Teachers and Principals *Katia Gonzáles*	113
10 Ethical Leadership in Times of Crises: Practical Guidelines and Suggestions *Jeffrey Glanz*	125
Future Directions	137
Index	143
About the Editor and Contributors	145

Series Editor's Introduction
Jeffrey Glanz

Why another book series on school leadership, and what does this particular series have to offer among the many fine books already published in the field of school and educational leadership?

Research over the past decade has confirmed what many educators, policymakers, think tanks, and others viscerally know—that leadership makes a difference for a host of dependent variables, including the most important one: student achievement. Additional research is needed, however, to more fully refine and uncover how school leaders make a difference in a host of other areas.

The answers to additional research questions will offer further legitimacy and draw greater attention to the field of educational leadership. The questions (which can prompt potential authors to submit a book proposal) include the following, among others:

- What are the relationships between personal beliefs, identity, and leadership?
- What effects do the continuing increased accountability and high-stakes testing have on teacher morale, principal self-efficacy, and student achievement?
- What additional information do we need about systems thinking and its relationship to school leadership?
- What are the specific gender differences related to leading schools?
- How might school leaders remain proactive in educational reform?
- What is the precise role played by school leaders in fostering inclusive educational practices?
- How is justice and equity for all best fostered by school leaders?
- What specific educational leadership strategies reduce the Black/White achievement gap?

- What can we learn from studying educational leadership from a multidisciplinary perspective?
- What role does leadership style have on effectiveness as a leader?
- How might school leaders implement an effective data-driven decision-making process in their schools?
- What are the critical factors affecting high performance among principals?
- What is the role of school leaders in reducing school violence?
- How do leadership practices positively influence school-community-university partnerships?
- What is the association between transformational leadership and teacher self-efficacy?
- How does shared leadership affect school morale and productivity?
- How do various types or forms of leadership impact organizational effectiveness?
- What are the social, cultural, political, and historical factors that influence the practice of educational leadership in different countries?
- How do leadership practices differ in differing contexts—social, cultural, or otherwise?
- What are the theoretical and practical differences among educational administration, management, supervision, and leadership?
- Why is an international perspective so critical for better understanding the challenges of leading schools in the twenty-first century?
- How can school leaders address race and identity, bias and privilege, and racialized current events?
- How can comparative research studies help us better understand educational leadership?
- What can we learn from studying educational leaders beyond the school level (e.g., district and Ministry of Education leaders)?
- To what extent does emotional labor impact educational leaders?
- How can principals encourage action research and other alternatives to supervision to enhance teachers' professional growth?
- How do school leaders effectively implement new technologies not only for the sake of technology but also to deepen learning and provide better support for teachers?
- What are the consequences of workload on school leaders (e.g., the principal) on effectiveness as a leader?
- What are the challenges that school leaders face in differing regional contexts?
- How do school leaders develop the skills and knowledge they need to understand teachers' and students' needs and effectively guide learning?

- How do effective school leaders balance administrative duties with instructional priorities?
- What new educational management strategies can help teachers better confront classroom behavioral issues?
- How do school leaders coordinate curriculum and instructional initiatives across schools?
- Given time and budget constraints, how can school leaders find the resources to support artful education (music, dance, creative writing, etc.) for all students?
- How do increased efforts to promote teacher leadership impact the work of principals and their assistants?
- What new innovative ideas can principals implement to deal with the increasingly complex landscape of curriculum today?
- How can principals support teacher-led professional development?
- What is the role of identity in fostering principal self-efficacy?
- How can school leaders help schools become more integral to their surrounding communities—and how can they better leverage community resources and connections to support their students and teachers?
- How can we better balance interest and work in instructional leadership with other important leadership responsibilities?
- How can districts support assistant principals and prepare new principals as they take the helm of the school?
- How do we recruit, induct, and sustain good principals?
- How can we best prepare future school leaders?

The series motto is framed after Kurt Lewin's famous statement, and I paraphrase, that there is no sound theory without practice and no good practice that is not framed on some theory. Most fundamentally, the R&L School Leadership Series is premised on the need to connect theory to practice. Each of the questions above relies on a sound theoretical base that has important, if not critical, relevance to the world of practice. This international series, in other words, reflects the latest cutting-edge theories and practices in school leadership that attempt to bridge the perennial divide between theory and practice.

Although we look to publish manuscripts that have relevance to an international audience, we will accept more localized research that might only be applicable in a specific context. We also encourage individuals who have completed a dissertation on a relevant topic to consider transforming their thesis into a book. Personally, my first book was framed on my dissertation, and I recall that the process was not so simple. If you think your work would have a larger appeal, I encourage you to consider a book with us. The manuscript, of course, must meet the rigors of academic research and address its possible impact on practice.

I welcome readers to join the effort to increase knowledge in our field and affect daily school practice by submitting a proposal on any of the topics mentioned above, or any other relevant ones. Feel free to communicate with me via email at yosglanz@gmail.com.

The series is sponsored and supported by two important people. Special acknowledgment is extended to Thomas Koerner, PhD (vice president and senior executive editor, Rowman and Littlefield Education) for his prompt feedback and encouragement. Special thanks to Carlie Wall, managing editor, for her expertise and support. Thanks to Meaghan Menzel, associate production editor, for professional facilitation of the production of my book in its final stages. With their assistance, I hope this series will receive wide acknowledgment for making a difference in the field of educational leadership.

* * *

Books already published in the Series:

Brown, K. (2011). *Preparing future leaders for social justice, equity, and excellence: Bridging theory and practice through a transformative andragogy* (first edition). Rowman and Littlefield.

Brown, K., and Shaked, H. (2018). *Preparing future leaders for social justice: Bridging theory and practice through a transformative andragogy* (second edition). Rowman and Littlefield.

Stader, D. (2012). *Leadership for a culture of school safety: Linking theory to practice.* Rowman and Littlefield.

Zepeda, S. J. (Ed.). (2018). *Making learning job-embedded: Cases from the field of educational leadership.* Rowman and Littlefield.

Zepeda, S. J. (Ed.). (2018). *The job-embedded nature of coaching: Lessons and insights for school leaders.* Rowman and Littlefield.

Zepeda, S. J. (Ed.). (2008). *Real world supervision: Adapting theory to practice.* Rowman and Littlefield.

Editor's Introduction

As series editor, I am excited to introduce a book in which I am serving as the editor: *Crisis and Pandemic Leadership: Implications for Meeting the Needs of Students, Teachers, and Parents*.

This work was inspired by the COVID-19 coronavirus pandemic that ravaged the world. As a result of this pandemic, schools have undergone monumental, unprecedented challenges that will likely affect and change school operations for many years. Teachers and administrators have scrambled to meet the needs of students, teachers, and parents amid the crisis.

This is not a book about the COVID-19 pandemic per se. Rather, contributors have used this global crisis to address topics in a number of areas that have implications that are universal. In preparing this work, I asked my contributors to consider these overarching, guiding questions:

1. Are schools prepared to deal with crises, in general, and what are the responsibilities and challenges of educational leaders in grappling with crises of all sorts?
2. And a bit more specifically, how can schools creatively design strategies to deal with challenges that arise in a crisis?

In this vein, our authors, using the COVID-19 pandemic as a frame of reference because of its currency, have discussed ways to sustain education for teachers and students in a variety of arenas, including sustaining the efficiency and effectiveness of the educational system (organization) as a whole, instructional delivery, teacher supervision and mentoring, confronting inequities that might become exacerbated in a crisis, and the overall impact on students, teachers, parents, and administrators.

We have assembled an array of diverse scholars who have thoughtfully addressed key issues in dealing with school crises from an educational leadership perspective. This book has framed certain challenges, certainly not all, as one book cannot do so. A perusal of the contents will demonstrate the geographic diversity of our contributors as well as the key topics each addresses.

School leaders must consider the type, nature, and particular circumstances unique to each crisis. Still, certain general principles or guidelines are common to all crises. We feel the topics we address will find relevance to researchers and practitioners in all situations at all times.

To encourage readers to introspect regarding issues presented, each chapter includes "Pre-Focus Guiding Questions," followed by a "Post-Note" to challenge readers to think about the ideas presented and to, in some cases, think about possible takeaway ideas they may put into practice.

I encourage readers to correspond with our contributors to further deepen the conversation about the role of school leaders amid crises of all sorts. We welcome your feedback and participation.

Jeffrey Glanz
March 2021

Chapter One

Building Sustainable Systems of Schooling in Turbulent Times

Big Ideas from the Sciences

Karolyn J. Snyder and Kristen M. Snyder

PRE-FOCUS GUIDING QUESTIONS

- What do you think is needed to build and sustain schools in turbulent times?
- What skills and dispositions are necessary for school leaders to effectively grapple with ever-evolving changes in the world that inevitably affect schools?
- In what ways can leaders embrace chaos and complexity to foster innovation during a crisis?
- How can networking and teaming foster conditions for adaptability in a crisis?

INTRODUCTION

The global COVID-19 pandemic of 2020 has shaken the very foundations of living everywhere around the globe, so much so that we are grasping at ways to recover and find a sustainable course for the future. The current pandemic unfolded at a time of dramatic complexity. Preparing students for life in a rapidly evolving global age of living and working, with its digital and virtual features, is challenging enough. But when an additional major crisis emerges, the situation becomes even more urgent. To deal with such challenges, educators need to reimagine schooling within the context of a larger ecosystem. Technology plays a critical role in this reimagination and has catapulted virtual schooling to the foreground, which opens up new worlds of learning opportunities.

What is expected in 2021 and beyond to reimagine school learning environments? The skills required for success as adults far exceed those of fifty years ago. For example, the World Economic Forum issued a complex new system of ideas in *21st Century Skills* (Soffel, 2016). The first group of skills includes the *foundation literacies* of reading, numeracy, science, Information and Communication Technologies (ICTs), and cultural and civic knowledge (the basics). The second group is identified as the *competencies* of critical thinking and problem solving, creativity, communication skills, and collaboration. The third group lists *character qualities,* which are newer expectations of workers, including curiosity, initiative, persistence, adaptability, leadership, and social and cultural awareness.

These complex skill sets of literacies, competencies, and character are now required of schools. However, the Organization for Economic Cooperation and Development's (OECD) Program for International Student Assessment (PISA) (2018) has called for yet another basic skill set in its testing of fifteen-year-old students. The original PISA exam in 1999 measured the quality of education in developed countries around the world for reading, math, and science. The new exam added the area of *global competence,* with three different levels as the focus for testing: global awareness, participation, and involvement (Ramos and Schleicher, 2018). The volume and complexity of learning demands on schools, compounded by the turbulence from a global pandemic and other possible future crises, prompt us to consider bold new avenues for designing schools as more durable, resilient, and adaptive learning systems. It is time to integrate digital living into classroom life and to intentionally reimagine schooling with a larger lens.

In this chapter, we offer "new ways of thinking" drawn from the sciences, especially from the evolution of physics over the last century. The change in physics began with Albert Einstein's ideas of relativity in space and time, which altered the way scientists think about how the universe works. For example, we now know that the universe is continuously expanding; it is a living system, with energy as its basic feature. It is within this perspective of relativity and quantum physics that the social and behavioral sciences emerged over the last century to help us understand how living systems become sustainable. The central lesson we can glean from the development of science is that the school is a living system that can and must adapt to changing times and crises. How it adapts is the focus of this chapter with implications for the work of school leaders (Snyder et al., 2008).

THE SCHOOLING CHALLENGE

Educators often need to update their professional capacities to meet the challenges of new student populations and new state requirements with emerging national and global environmental conditions. Such flexibility is more urgent amid a major school crisis. The concepts of *emergence, unfolding,* and *evolution* are common to the growth of natural systems, which is a fresh way of thinking about how schools emerge over time and how they can adapt to crises. As living systems, schools exist in communities with changing demographics, and new cultural, economic, political, and social conditions. Change is inevitable, and school leaders of the twenty-first century must be prepared to adapt.

Another challenging issue for school leaders is the nature of change and its evolution. Physicists tell us that *connections* are essential building blocks for generating the energy necessary for continuous improvement, renovation, and transformation. Energy, as informed by physics, is the essential force in the universe for stimulating continuous expansion and development, and the most vital and reliable force for shaping schooling in turbulent times. How might schools build more energy for growth from connections?

In the next section, six *Big Ideas* from the sciences are presented with lessons for leaders in learning to foster more sustainable school development. Later in the chapter, we will highlight a private pre-K-8th grade school to illustrate the power of using these *Big Ideas* and the connections made when professionals learn to function as "one community," in which the responsibilities for continuous improvement are shared by all.

SIX LESSONS FROM THE SCIENCES

Let us consider the *Big Ideas* from physics that are guideposts for fashioning new learning systems amid crises of all sorts. The six ideas are visualized in figure 1.1. We suggest that these big ideas hold great promise for educators, globally, to launch systems of innovation and sustainability by embracing disequilibrium and building systems for flexibility and resilience.

Big Idea #1: Energy Builds from Connections

Change in natural systems evolves from continuous connections with the external environment, as well as from within the system itself. The quality of connections matters, however, for negative and positive connections promote altogether different levels of energy and outcomes (Snyder et al., 2008). For example, negative connections build negatively, whereas positive connections build positively. And, where there are no connections, there is little energy generated and virtually no growth. When the connections become dense, the system develops its own energy system and direction for growth.

The principle underlying this *Big Idea* is that negative connections build negatively, and precipitate more negative connections and outcomes, whereas dense positive connections generate a positive energy system as it pursues its positive outcomes. The challenge for educators is to bring the message of positive energy with positive connections to the conscious and operational

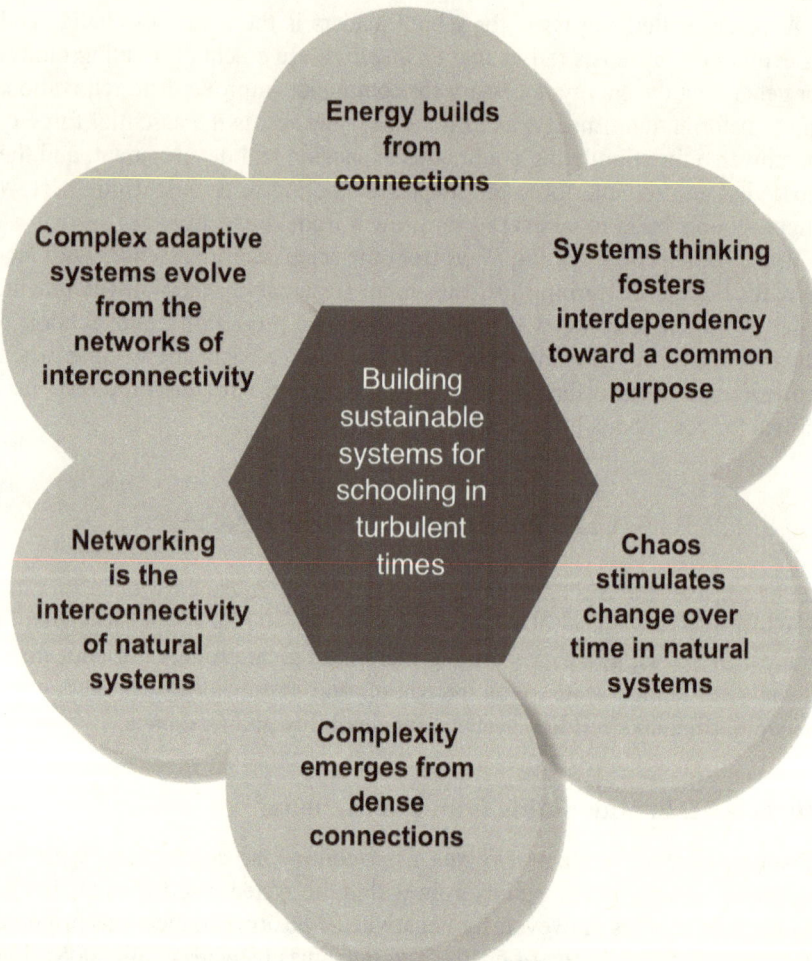

Figure 1.1. Six big ideas from the sciences. *Source*: Karolyn J. Snyder and Kristen M. Snyder

levels at a systemic level, thus affecting all school constituents.

Big Idea #2: Systems-Thinking Fosters Interdependency and Common Purpose

Physicists observe that the emergence of systems-thinking is a profound revolution in modern history, for it causes us to shift our approach to life from "fixing the problems in machines" to "promoting growth in living systems" (Capra and Luisi, 2016). A systems view of life creates the mindset that everyone is working together toward a common purpose. A systems approach is a shift toward a multidisciplinary strategy for development, is relationship-oriented, embraces mapping possibilities rather than evaluation systems, and measures success in quality, values, and process. Systems-thinking can alter how we think about change and building sustainable school programs and services (Shaked and Schechter, 2017).

In our work with schools, we created a model for educators to think about linking the work systems in school life around a common purpose (Snyder and Anderson, 1986) with a focus on student success (Snyder et al., 2008). By linking and coordinating the work subsystems of leadership, organization, performance, programs, and management, educators begin to shift their thinking and actions toward new interdependent pathways for achieving common goals and meeting student needs. As the interdependence of functions and role groups take hold in a school, the climate and culture of work take on new importance. Educators become increasingly aware that in collaborative environments positive connections spawn more positive outcomes.

Big Idea #3: Chaos Stimulates Change over time in Natural Systems

If a school is a living system with interdependent functions that work toward common purposes, what then is the nature of growth and change over time? Scientists began to study the change in different kinds of natural systems, beginning with mathematics (Gleick, 1987). They soon became aware that change is not predictable, nor is it linear, and yet it follows patterns of consistency within its own system (i.e., forests grow and die as forests) (Snyder et al., 2008). We have observed that educators find relief from the positive impact that chaos can have on their school's growth process. Eventually, we developed the *Chaos Theory of Change,* which is based on the essential patterns that scientists found in natural systems. This perspective on growth over time is natural, for we experience it in our daily lives; we are not machines but rather living systems that need continuous feeding to grow in healthy ways. *The Chaos Theory of Change* consists of four ideas:

1. Living systems grow in relation to changes within their local environment: For example, different regions of the world experienced varying degrees of cases and numbers of deaths from the COVID-19 pandemic, each having an impact on schooling locally.
2. Disequilibrium emerges from the environment to disturb the natural system. Disequilibrium is a good thing, for it pushes the natural system (a school) to the edge so that change must be considered if the system is to survive. Disturbances in the environment (the pandemic) create an avalanche of local explorations into how schooling might continue.
3. Energy for addressing challenges inherent in disequilibrium emerges from connections, information, and resources. Building a strong system of internal and external connections is essential to offset the negative impact of disequilibrium. For example, not all new pandemic-generated systems of learning that emerged around the world were of equal value to students. The leadership challenge is to determine that the strength of the newly built energy system has the potential to offset the influence of the disequilibrium source.
4. The edge of chaos is resolved through self-organization. The essential idea is that things do not fall apart when disequilibrium threatens to disturb the status quo. Rather, by building energy systems for gathering resources and studying information, new ideas and energy naturally emerge to address the challenges. Self-organization naturally kicks in so that the system (of schooling) does not fall apart but rather emerges onto a path of sustainability. As a result, new systems that have sustainability potential eventually evolve naturally. The cycle of disequilibrium to equilibrium becomes the normal dance of life in a school that is viewed as a living system, and comfort grows as educators come to understand the power of disequilibrium, connection systems, and self-organization.

Big Idea #4: **Complexity Emerges from Dense Connections**

A fundamental feature of living systems is that complexity grows naturally, and it emerges over time, following its design. Systems-thinking naturally leads to greater complexity, which strengthens a system's cohesiveness and resilience (Buchanan, 2002). As complex systems grow more complex, they never reverse and become simple. Since complex natural systems grow in a nonlinear fashion and move quickly and unpredictability, surprises emerge. Surprise becomes routine from the multidimensional life that exists within a system with a nonlinear set of rules. New professional capacities emerge to address the growing complexity and surprises of school life.

Big Idea #5: Networking is the Interconnectivity of Natural Systems

Networking within an organization is the natural result of systems-thinking, which involves a growing connection of elements within and outside the organization and the understanding of disequilibrium and self-organization in the organic process of growth. Human networks have existed since the beginning of civilization, although they have been studied as science only since the 1960s with the "Six Degrees of Separation" phenomenon (Barabasi, 2016). After decades of promoting systems-thinking and the interdependency of work systems, we now suggest that the next level of organizational development is network-thinking, which is the interconnectedness of everything. Technology platforms have fueled networking to function well along with more traditional hierarchical structures, a new norm (Ferguson, 2017).

Scientists find that dense networks are more durable than simple networks due to the strength of connections. A network grows from within itself, rather than from external forces, as it responds continuously to changing conditions and opportunities. Ideas about networking within organizations are only beginning to take shape. As networks emerge, leaders share ideas and power comes from the unification of goals that focus on the crisis at hand. Another finding is this: the more complex the network, the fewer fluctuations emerge to disrupt its performance and growth. The greater a network's complexity, the more stable it becomes (Buchanan, 2002).

Big Idea #6: Complex Adaptive Systems Evolve from Networks of Interconnectivity

The concept of complex adaptive systems (CAS) emerged from the science of chaos theory and has become a metaphor for living systemically and sustainably (Holland, 1995). Highly developed complex systems, and networks of systems, easily adapt to changing conditions. A dynamic network of many agents work in parallel, constantly acting and reacting to what other agents are doing and learning. Control is decentralized as agents continuously learn from each other and the environment about change and possibilities. Rules change continuously in the adaptation process as agents learn, respond to, and pursue their system's sustainability. Supporting CAS becomes a coordinated effort between a school's hierarchy and its networks functioning as a new kind of learning system.

In the next section, we aim to translate the somewhat abstract ideas articulated above and demonstrate their practicality in a school. We worked with Corbett Preparatory School (CPS) to explore these six big ideas in practice. Through the stories of the leadership and selected teachers, we illustrate the manner in which the staff and community embraced the disequilibrium of the pandemic and turned the school and its systems for teaching and learning upside down. Along the journey, we identify some of the key processes and tools they used to address the crisis. In doing so, their capacity to meet the needs of students, teachers, parents, and communities increased dramatically.

CORBETT PREPARATORY SCHOOL: A CASE EXAMPLE

Corbett Preparatory School at IDS, an independent day school in Tampa, Florida, has become a continuous award-winning school for decades, recognized for its strong positive culture and approaches to teaching and learning (www.corbettprep.com). CPS is also a school that is built upon the strong foundations of *Big Ideas* we shared from the sciences that enabled educators to rapidly become a complex adaptive system in the COVID-19 environment. We highlight part of their journey here to illustrate how the *Big Ideas* from science can be applied in schools.

When the pandemic hit Florida in March 2020, CPS, like all other schools, began to face the basic question: *How can schooling continue?* During spring 2020, CPS remained open as a virtual school following the same weekly schedule as on-campus schooling. While very successful as an innovation, in hindsight, leaders and teachers realized this learning model was not sustainable in the long run. If the school campus was to open in the fall, the learning needed to be reimagined to retain the school's core values of a safe and nurturing environment for everyone.

In July 2020, a new headmaster was instated at CPS. This change, although planned before the pandemic, caused a kind of disequilibrium in the school that would later be used to stimulate a new mindset. Over the summer months, the school's leadership team built a strong energy system that connected the school and community in dynamic new ways. In August 2020, CPS opened its doors with a hybrid model for teaching and learning that was designed around the school's core values of team teaching and cooperative learning, communication, and community. The results from this innovation were so striking that communities across the region celebrated CPS for its remarkable achievement.

The Case

It was July 7, and a new day dawned on the grounds of CPS. The headmaster of twenty-four years, Joyce, internationally recognized for her innovation in education and designing an award-winning school, was ready to assume a new role. It was time to welcome the new headmaster, Nick. This transition, however, was met with an unprecedented crisis, COVID-19. The school was not in session. The looming question was how CPS would continue to serve its students, parents, and community with a quality education that was safe and sustainable over time. The school was well-known for its strong humanistic values and student-centered learning (Cohen, 2003), team teaching (Snyder and Anderson, 1986), respect for individuals and their unique talents, as well as resilience and active community involvement in the school.

As a new head of school, Nick realized that the old paradigm of traditional solutions to which he was accustomed was no longer of use. If school was to open, he needed a new set of lenses and a new approach to schooling. Joining him were two other leaders who had worked in the school before, Mike (associate headmaster) and Jenn (middle school division leader). The leadership team decided that given the current crisis, teaching and learning had to be reimagined. Nick explained, "It's like we are building a puzzle without the outside pieces. You just keep building, because the puzzle keeps moving depending on what angle you are going at. There are many challenges."

Mike and Jenn, along with Joyce, the former headmaster, were at the school when the pandemic first hit. "We have battle scars from our experience in the spring," shared Mike. He continued, "We did our best with what we had at the time, and like all schools, we learned from our experiences, which informed the design of a new approach."

During July, the core leadership team met for twelve hours a day to build a sixty-page back-to-school strategic plan. Their work was guided by a strong understanding about the need to embrace a systems approach to draw on the strength of the schools existing work structures, systems, and values. The initial days were spent walking through the school's facilities observing, recording, and discussing the changes necessary to make the school safe. The core leadership team partnered with the IT staff, realizing they were critical to reimagining teaching and learning. As part of their strategy, the leaders benchmarked with twenty other schools within the Florida Council of Independent Schools (FCIS) to learn from one another about best practices to grapple with the unpredictable reality of the current crisis. Networking, they knew, would be critical to their success. Mike commented, "Listening and sharing with others gave us a kind of ambidexterity to redesign the school quickly."

Redesigning the school was not only about affecting structural changes. The core values and principles of team teaching and cooperative learning served as the glue and backbone to their plan. Anchoring the plan in the school's values was paramount to enable new solutions to emerge from chaos. Moreover, the leadership team recognized that their success was dependent upon trust, communication, and involvement of everyone if, in the words of one of the administrators, "we were going to pull off a miracle." Mike shared,

> On July 15, a week after Nick started, we had a faculty meeting, face to face and on zoom. The purpose was to create the realization that we are going to try and pull off something that we had never done before, for which we needed everyone's help. Thirdly, we needed to demonstrate with technology the dimension of our plan to show how teachers were going to teach.

Building on the foundation of shared leadership in the school was one of the key elements that helped Corbett Preparatory School radically transform the structures of teaching and learning to a blended learning model. The network and interconnectedness of the division teams as a pedagogical and organizational system fostered the conditions necessary for adaptability. Cultures of trust, understanding the system-as-a-whole, and clarity of common purpose were being set in motion to respond to the chaos and disequilibrium caused by the pandemic. Nick explained,

> Originally when I came here, I thought we needed to add a couple of traditional roles because we are so flat. But soon I began to realize the power of the existing network model and shared leadership among the Division Leaders, who knew best what is going on in the classroom. This has been critical to our ability to build a new puzzle without knowing the parameters more than safety and kids first.

The school had a strong culture of shared leadership, which was used to support adaptability in the school. One of the teachers shared that, "when we began to meet as a division planning group, everyone volunteered ideas for what they thought was needed. Each teacher and aide spontaneously volunteered to take on tasks for the whole division. Something new was happening . . . it was spontaneous." Mike also shared that involving the teachers and division teams early on "was vital, not only for buy-in but for input. We got so many new comments and ideas from the teachers, which became version two of the plan."

The school's leadership continued to build on the strength and energy from the various collaborations. Total staff engagement and the school's strong orientation to continuous improvement were important ingredients to help the staff regroup and to adapt their structures and teaching in fundamentally new ways for the COVID-19 environment. Building on this orientation, the leadership extended collaboration to include additional groups, typically outside the planning process, among them parents, a school board task force of lawyers, physicians, Center for Disease Control (CDC) officials, technology consultants, and even the buildings' grounds crew. Through the collaboration, communication was open, transparent, quick, and centered around the school's values and a common purpose.

It was becoming apparent that the ability and readiness of the school to adapt to a pandemic was due in large part to following the natural laws of science stressing a systems view of the school as an organization, the importance of establishing and fostering connections to build energy and resilience, to enhance and maintain lines of open communications, and to strengthen all networks with a shared vision and common values.

The result of the numerous meetings and feedback loops from teachers, parents, and board members was a new "back-to-school plan" that was designed to ensure safety from the virus, be flexible to meet the variety of student needs, and allow the school to stay open to adaptation over time. The initial prototype was designed, centered on blended learning models to deliver education simultaneously on campus and remotely via Zoom to maintain two core principles of the school's pedagogical practices: team teaching and cooperative learning.

The plan for reopening school was to offer a hybrid model in which teaching teams would carry out their classes with both remote learners and classroom-based learners simultaneously. Arranging this approach required changes in the on-site school facilities, ongoing professional development (PD) for teachers, and rethinking the way technology was used in the classroom. It also required a mind shift among the staff and students, which advanced them into a "Digital Culture" (Snyder, 2007), reflecting an integration of pedagogy, communication, technology, and organizational systems. With little time for PD, however, teachers worked in their division teams to redesign their teaching and prepare for a whole new reality.

In Table 1.1, we highlight some of the changes that took place, using the Digital Culture model framework: Pedagogy, Communication, Technology, and Organization. A perusal of the table demonstrates the initiatives in each area.

The shift to the digital culture (table 1.1) illustrates ways in which the leaders were able to respond to the pandemic and adapt the school quickly. Technological and administrative solutions were designed through teams of people at all levels of the school. Decisions were grounded in the school's principles of team teaching and cooperative learning. And the importance of communication informed decisions about how to insure good, sound quality given that everyone was wearing masks, and a sense of one community and being together despite the distance. Moreover, the organizational systems such as scheduling, planning, and leading were adapted to meet the needs of the learning environment. As Nick shared,

Table 1.1.

Pedagogy	Technology	Communication	Organization
Team teaching and cooperative learning were the foundations around which technological solutions were designed.	iPads and tripods were used to set up Zoom stations on movable iPad tripods to maintain flexibility and student-centered learning.	Teachers wore microphones over their face masks; at-home student photos were displayed on the classroom whiteboard.	The buildings and grounds were all cleaned; furniture and learning arrangements were modified. New sinks and walkway gates were added to self-contained student groups.
Kids were put into cooperative learning groups in seventh-grade English, combining classroom-based and remote learners in learning communities.	Teacher planning and scheduling have moved from paper to a shared online document and they communicate with parents daily to get feedback.	Canvas LMS was used to communicate and share information; Zoom was used to communicate synchronously during the day.	The flow of students was changed: Students remained in the classroom, and teachers moved from room to room. For example, the arts came to the classroom; the science teachers had a lab cart that they took with them.
Seventh graders functioned in Zoom breakout rooms, integrating in-class and at-home kids into groups to discuss short stories.	New fire walls were added to the campus, with increased broadband width and access points.	At home, students photo copy their work and send it to CANVASS, or upload it to email.	Desks were spaced either six feet apart, or plexiglass partitions were inserted between students at tables and desk combinations.

I recently read an article in which the CEOs of major companies were asked the question: What made your company truly enter the digital age? There was only one answer among the many participants: COVID. And that is true for us. COVID allowed us to push forward pedagogically as well as a community with parents. The big questions that guided us were how do we bring learning to all kids that is safe, fun and nurturing, and at the same time not lose our values of individual difference?; how do we communicate everything digitally?; and how do we maintain and build relationships purely online? We realized that we needed to ensure that our technological and human systems remain adaptive.

CONCLUSION

This chapter has focused on the importance for school leaders to create strong internal systems of work that are interdependent and interconnected, centered around a common purpose and set of values to be responsive to changing conditions, including crises. Corbett Preparatory School has been identified by local news networks as a beacon of light amid the pandemic for its ability to change the "school on a dime," while maintaining a commitment to its students, teachers, parents, and community. The mindset of the school leaders, and those that work at all levels of the school, were instrumental for building new energy systems out of chaos.

Rather than isolating everyone for a new pandemic-minded learning environment for the August reopening of school, the leadership team built upon their foundational values of collaboration, teaming, and networking. Everyone participated in designing parts of the new model of learning while sharing responsibilities and accountability. The school's leadership team became a vital support system for improved teaching and learning. The CPS innovation was framed on the collective talents of many constituents to create an adaptive learning system using the school's core values of community and working together to innovate, test, and modify practice.

Listening to Nick, the headmaster, reflect on the sustainability of the school's adaptation, he shared that, "sustainability requires that we have open communications, clarity of purpose, clarity of roles, and a network of teams who are all working in the same direction." And for Mike, the associate headmaster, "one of the big lessons for me about leading in a pandemic is to trust your gut. We still need information to inform our decisions, but sometimes we don't have it. We need to be open and honest with ourselves and with one another that we don't always have the answers. We also have learned about the power of networking: sharing information between schools and within our school community to adapt to the complexity of the crisis and still maintain our core values."

We have indicated in this chapter that lessons from the sciences can liberate school leaders to ignite energy for reimagining and reshaping schools no matter how turbulent the times. The sustainability of schooling as a public or private service depends on how well networks are built that become complex adaptive systems of learning for a school's development. The future of schooling depends on bold leadership that embraces systems-thinking, living on the edge of chaos, and network-thinking to become adaptive no matter the crisis.

POST-NOTE

- Which ideas from the sciences resonated the most with you? How would you as principal implement them in your school?
- What are some obstacles to implementing some of the ideas presented in this chapter? How can you as principal work to overcome them?
- What specific lessons have you garnered about dealing with a crisis from the case of Corbett Preparatory School? Why or why not would these lessons work in your school?
- Clearly, a crisis of any sort can cause disequilibrium. How can systems-thinking help deal with this situation?

REFERENCES

Barabasi, A. L. (2016). *Network science.* Cambridge University Press.

Buchanan, M. (2002). *Small worlds: A ground-breaking theory of networks.* W. W. Norton and Company.

Capra, F., and Luisi, P. L. (2016). *The systems view of life: A unifying vision.* Cambridge University Press.

Cohen, D. (2003). *It's all about kids: Every child deserves a "Teacher of the Year."* Independent Day School.

Ferguson, N. (2017). *The square and the tower: Networks and power, from the Freemasons to Facebook.* Penguin Press.

Gleick, J. (1987). *Chaos: Making a new science.* Penguin Books.

Holland, J. H. (1995). *Hidden order: How adaptation builds complexity.* Basic Books.

OECD/PISA (2018). http://www.oecd.org/pisa/.

Ramos, G., and Schleicher, A. (2018). PISA: Preparing our youth for an inclusive and sustainable world—The OECD/PISA global competence framework. OECD (Organization for Economic Community Development). http://www.oecd.org/pisa/aboutpisa/Global-competency-for-an-inclusive-world.pdf#.

Shaked, H., and Schechter, C. (2017). *Systems thinking for school leaders: Holistic leadership for excellence in education.* Springer.

Snyder, K. J., and Anderson, R. H. (1986). *Managing productive schools: Toward an ecology.* Harcourt, Brace and Jovanovich.

Snyder, K. J., Acker-Hocevar, M., and Snyder, K. M. (2008). *Living on the edge of chaos: Leading Schools into the global age.* ASQ: The Quality Press.

Snyder, K. M. (2007). The digital culture and "Peda-Socio," transformation. *Seminar .net*, 3(1), 1–15.

Soffel, J. (2016). What are the 21st century skills every student needs? World Economics Forum. https.//www.weforum.org/agenda/2016/03/21st-century-skills-future-jobs-students/.

Chapter Two

Educating In and Beyond a Crisis
An Australian Perspective
Lisa Vinnicombe

PRE-FOCUS GUIDING QUESTIONS

- In your leadership preparatory program, to what extent were you taught about the best ways to deal with a school-related crisis?
- What are some essential leadership qualities and characteristics to effectively manage a crisis?
- How has the COVID-19 pandemic experience changed your perceptions of school leadership?
- After having experienced a major school crisis, what lessons have you learned? What might you do differently in the future to better prepare for any crisis?

INTRODUCTION

In times of crisis and uncertainty, school leaders are charged with the responsibility of leading their school community through turbulent times and managing school operations in a climate of rapid and unexpected change and sudden increases in demand on resources (Clarke, 2016; Smith and Riley, 2012; Tran et al., 2020). The human side of leadership is at no time more called upon than in a time of crisis. Effective school leaders realize that remaining sensitive to the needs of people (students, parents, teachers, other administrators) is a critical disposition, especially in times of crisis (Bolman and Deal, 2017). In a crisis, school leaders realize the potential threat to the well-being of the community, and, therefore, the sense of urgency to deal with it is pervasive.

In a crisis, school principals are challenged with the task of mobilizing all members of the staff and to encourage higher levels of autonomy and initiative to deal effectively with unpredictable changes. Principals leading through and beyond crises recognize the need to acknowledge the professionalism of their staff and demonstrate this belief by trusting the staff with more responsibility. Thus, they tolerate and even encourage initiative and innovation (Jaroensutiyotin et al., 2019). Decision-making, with this mindset, becomes, at least in part, a shared responsibility of key elements in the school community.

This chapter explores the imperatives of school leadership during a major crisis but also discusses lessons learned and ways school leadership may change in a post-crisis environment (Cloninger, 2018). On this latter focus, the chapter will consider tensions that will likely challenge school leaders after having experienced a traumatic crisis but will indicate that possibilities and opportunities for creative and innovative leadership naturally emerge only if the leader is introspective and forward-looking.

Discussion in this chapter will consider crises from a uniquely Australian perspective. In understanding and dealing with crises, one must recognize the importance of the context in which the crisis emerges as well as the particular problems of that context. For instance, although inequities in education exist everywhere, they may be exacerbated in a particular context and, therefore, need special attention and emphasis from the school leader. In Australia, during the COVID-19 pandemic, for example, the impact of the crisis on young people was particularly marked. Hence, school leaders had to grapple with issues unique to their particular context. We will consider the implications of a major crisis for young people and their mental health and the optimal characteristics that school leaders should possess to effectively deal with them.

AN AUSTRALIAN CONTEXT

When the news finally broke that the world was officially in a global pandemic, Australia was experiencing a crisis of its own—one not uncommon but certainly unprecedented in its history. Brisbane was heating up unseasonably while Sydney became engulfed in smoke. The heat waves that they experienced were unprecedented; people were confused and uncertain about the meaning of this weather crisis, about what it foreshadowed, and a sense of foreboding hung over the country and, in particular, the eastern states.

As the summer drew nearer, reports came in of wildlife simply giving up and laying down defeated in the face of the extremities of weather. Then, with little warning, bushfires along the southeast coast in Victoria and New South

Wales burned with a new and terrifying ferocity, with an awful intensity and relentlessness. In a country known for searing, dry summers and drought, fires are a constant threat; however, the most recent situation was extreme.

While the bushfires continued to rage, there was another crisis looming, a global crisis: The COVID-19 pandemic swept across Australia as it did across the whole world, with little opportunity for those bushfire-ravaged communities already in ruin to restock and recover before facing the next challenge. Schools that had been impacted by the fires and were already severely challenged, shifted to a new level of urgency. Moreover, there was little to reference and learn from, as it became apparent that many policymakers, including school officials, were surprised, overwhelmed, and ill-prepared to deal with these near-simultaneous crises. However, leaders at all levels of society realized, in general, that the urgency of crises, their unpredictability, their ambiguity, their threat to stability and equilibrium, and their high probability for negative impact were challenges that had to be met (Jaroensutiyotin et al., 2019; Smith and Riley, 2012; Topper and Lagadec 2013). For schools, the extraordinary difficulty posed demonstrates the complexity of leadership in crisis and suggests a broad-ranging skill set is necessary to effectively manage crises.

Crisis Leadership Guidelines in Australia

In Australia, school leadership models exist that recognize the unique challenges of crisis leadership. The Australian Institute of School Leadership (AITSL) describes the work of the school principal in the following way:

> Principals are able to embrace uncertain, complex, and challenging contexts and work with others to seek creative and innovative solutions that support quality outcomes for all . . . The principal works in a complex, challenging and changing environment, leading and managing the school of today, ever-conscious of the needs of tomorrow. (AITSL, p. 6)

Further, AITSL stipulates a range of leadership requirements of the school principal; they must:

- possess vision
- behave with integrity
- model values and ethical perspectives
- inspire and motivate
- prepare for challenges
- make informed decisions
- understand the practice and theory of contemporary leadership (AITSL, p. 5)

The AITSL guidelines also recognize that leaders must possess a skill set that is directly crisis-related and, as a result, they added certain characteristics in leaders that are deemed crucial to effectively manage a crisis. These include:

- the ability to cope and thrive on ambiguity
- the ability to respond flexibly and quickly
- the tenacity and optimism to persevere when all seems lost
- a capacity to think laterally and creatively

Given that Australia deals with weather-related crises annually, policymakers and boards of education realize the high demand for leadership that is adaptive (Heifetz et al., 2009) and that is responsive to an ever-increasing complex world outside of schools. The current "dual crisis" calls for leaders who can think creatively and innovatively amid the uncertainty caused by significant change and disruption (Jaroensutiyotin et al., 2019).

The School Response in Australia

Australia is a vast continent, with most of the population living on and around the east and southeast coast. The center is mostly desert, the distances between places make travel extremely difficult, and the states and territories generally act as small countries within one larger country. Schools in Australia represent an extremely diverse society, and students come to school from very different backgrounds and neighborhoods with a vast range of skills and experiences; therefore, there is no particular leadership model that fits all needs.

A quick snapshot of how the federal government managed the recent global crisis concerning schools was to agree in the first instance to a set of National Principles for school education, then direct the states and territories to take individual responsibility for their schools, informed by official and expert health and education advice. This led to a range of consequences across the country for schools. Some schools went into immediate lockdown. Some encouraged the older students to continue at school, while others allowed students of essential workers to attend. Most schools, though, closed, but then reopened, and then once again closed, with the situation repeating over time. Overall, it was messy and inconsistent, with each jurisdiction trying to keep up with daily and weekly reports to schools, communities, and families.

Compounding these difficulties was the fact that communications were erratic and often nonexistent. School leaders were charged with the task of deciphering government mandates and changing policies and communicating various news briefs and updates to students, staff, and families. For the most part, schools lacked the infrastructure needed to go seamlessly into immediate, unplanned lockdown as well as a shift to remote schooling. It was unchartered territory and a very complex and complicated transition.

It became readily apparent, given the excessive strains on Australia's educational system, that the crisis impelled educators to explore alternative ways to lead and deal with seemingly intractable problems of all sorts: educational, pedagogical, social, and emotional (Cloninger, 2018). Also clear was that standard operating procedures of the past decades that relied on conforming to a very linear model of education that was resource-dependent and spoke to a post-industrial need for young people to join a workforce were no longer viable. Schools across Australia rapidly transitioned into remote learning, yet so many of the structures and frameworks that had been relied on for years suddenly seemed obsolete, inadequate, and impractical. It is within this context that the task of principals was to mobilize their staff with a sense of urgency to provide an educational environment conducive to learning.

THE NEW IMPERATIVE FOR SCHOOL LEADERS: MENTAL HEALTH AND WELL-BEING

There are many aspects of the educational process affected by a severe crisis that may need emphasis and attention. However, the remaining discussion will focus on an area of concern often omitted when confronting a dramatic school and community crisis and the kind of school leadership that is necessary. School leaders were not aware, at least initially, of the degree to which students would adapt to a sudden transition to remote learning. Working solely from home, without their friends, the comfort of classrooms, and the security of a teacher physically present yielded a crisis, in and of itself, that was not foreseen.

Perhaps the most lasting impact of school closures due to the COVID-19 crisis in Australia was the uncertainty around the mental health of young people. As is evidenced in current literature, research indicates the harmful, lasting effects on young people who school remotely for long periods (Sonneman and Goss, 2020). Schools provide a sense of stability for many young people. It is a place where they feel safe and secure, and a place that provides them with a structure and routine that they need (Aguliera and Nightengale-Lee, 2020). For many students, the pandemic represented a traumatic time of uncertainty, ambiguity, tension, and unease.

Evidence suggests that school leaders needed both the resources and knowledge to map out a mentally healthy life model for young people and then share this model with policymakers to ensure that schools could be adequately resourced to provide needed supports to fend off potential mental health concerns among students, including anxiety, depression, self-harm, and suicide (Kutcher and Wei, 2020). The pandemic crisis reinforced the importance for schools to provide a safe, stable place for young people (George et al., 2018).

Faced with an unfamiliar and uncertain future, school leaders needed to refine their models of leadership to focus much more than in the past on confronting and providing assistance to young students hurled suddenly into a situation that would impact not only their learning and achievement but also, more urgently, their social-emotional health. School leaders need a new or, at least, refined or redirected model of leadership that seeks to expand curricula to focus on nonacademic concerns that directly impact learning (Cohen, 2016). Principals, for instance, need competency and experience as instructional leaders, but they also must have a nuanced understanding of the correlation between good mental health and learning capacity. Their ability to coordinate and align the two as part of their leadership responsibilities is crucial, especially during a school crisis (Parks, 2005).

Several school leaders in Australia were cognizant of their need to attend to issues of mental health and well-being due to the unique dual-crises confronting large areas of the country. They prepared, for example, by altering the school structure and organization by implementing mental health professional development webinars and seminars where feasible. They realigned their leadership model to include a close examination of curricula for students, initiatives when recruiting new faculty, and providing for and leading programs around mental health issues, not only for students but also for teachers and families. These leaders realized the long-lasting effects of trauma that many experienced during the lockdowns of 2020 and foresaw the ramifications for students and others.

Extant school leadership models support such thinking and practice. Schools are complex organizations with a multitude of needs to suit the vast range of clientele. School leadership models that break away from linear types of thinking to more inclusionary models that encompass a broad range of areas and concerns within a school are better suited for leading during a crisis. These school leaders realize that within the organizational structure of the school there needs to be flexibility and creativity that reflects all diverse populations, never ignoring or placing the needs of students on the back burner. These leaders understand the value of new models of leadership in the twenty-first century that rely on collaborative practices (Hargreaves and Fullan, 2012) and view principals as integral change agents who take into consideration in their model of leadership all the diverse constituents in a school community (Fullan, 1993; 2005).

With this new, more encompassing model of leadership, school leaders of the future will acknowledge the crucial social role of schools. Particularly, they will reference the social needs of young people (Shaked, 2020) and ensure that the organizational structure of the school caters to the needs of young people to interact, engage, and learn in healthy ways. Parenthetically, the point here is not to dismiss the fact that good principals of the past were indeed cognizant of student needs; they certainly were aware. However, especially amid serious crises, a refined model of leadership is needed to reemphasize and realign attention to students' emotional and social well-being. The model of leadership advocated here, first and foremost, aligns the academic needs of young people with their emotional health and well-being. For policymakers, this leadership model requires additional resources, both financial and personnel. Parenthetically, in Victoria, the government has already committed to providing such support to schools as a result of the COVID-19 crisis.

Influenced by a major crisis, this new imperative for school leaders does not ignore the well-being of teachers. On the contrary, it appreciates the emotional labor of the work of teaching and acknowledges and supports teachers' work during and beyond a crisis (see, e.g., Bodenheimer and Shuster, 2020; Gallant, 2013; Gallant and Riley, 2013; Hargreaves, 1998; Noddings, 1992). The well-being of students is dependent on the well-being of teachers, who, it has been suggested, "engage in emotional labour as a routine part of their jobs" (Bodenheimer and Shuster, 2020, p. 69). School leaders during and after the pandemic recognize that teacher health is crucial to sustaining their capacity to enact a high level of care for their students.

TENSIONS IN A POST-CRISIS MILIEU

Following a dramatic crisis, school leadership is challenged by several tensions:

- tensions of balancing students operating in a highly competitive environment with positive mental health capacities;
- tensions between student autonomy and the need for teamwork and positive social learning experiences;
- ongoing digital tensions between balancing digital technology as a twenty-first-century skill and minimizing the risk of the negative impact of the digital world (George et al., 2018);
- tensions between preserving culture and tradition while also becoming global citizens; and
- tensions of school leaders in grappling with future, often unpredictable crises.

These tensions also include the awareness and attention to the almost inevitable inequities and uneven opportunities available to students across Australia, both in curriculum and outside of the classroom. A key implication of the most recent crisis is the importance for school leaders to address this equity imbalance to ensure that all students, regardless of background, have the opportunity to succeed. For school leaders, this may mean restructuring the school and considering innovative ways of extending students' interests and capabilities beyond the standardized curriculum, while still addressing the traditional means of accessing higher education opportunities through the established examination process.

The lockdown exposed the reality that schools are an unequal playing field and provided compelling evidence of an "opportunity gap" (Darling-Hammond, 2010, p. 28) for many students who lacked access to resources (Shaked, 2020). Technology was the most prominent and obvious of those resources, but analysis revealed that during the lockdown teachers also struggled to address the limited capacity for many students to access a satisfactory work environment outside of school. For school leaders, this will continue to be a challenge during and beyond the pandemic.

CONCLUSION

"The COVID-19 pandemic has created undeniable chaos. At the same time, it has unleashed a wealth of energy in innovative, collaborative, and laser-focused problem-solving" (Hargreaves and Fullan, 2020, p. 9). Leadership in crisis calls for more than a reactionary, problem-solving approach. The most recent worldwide pandemic crisis has raised some compelling arguments for leadership models in Australia to consider the importance of mental health and well-being, of striving for a resilient and thriving student population, and of restructuring the school so that well-being and emotional needs are prioritized alongside the academic curriculum needs of the students (Egan, 2008).

Schools are multifunctional institutions, serving many roles in communities. For students, school is more than just a place of learning, a trajectory into work and higher education. For young people, school is where they develop their social selves, where they form friendships and contacts that may last years, where they develop the "soft" skills of teamwork, collaboration, sharing, communication, mindfulness, creativity, and cultural sensitivity (Shaked, 2020). For many, it is a safe place—where often, home is neither safe nor welcoming. For those students, the school contacts are crucial, even life-saving, and losing those contacts for even a short time can have disastrous consequences.

School leadership plays a pivotal role in navigating crises and their consequences. Leadership that focuses on students' mental health needs as a priority is essential. Crisis and pandemic leadership involves, in the case presented about Australia, a concern for student well-being, on greater self-understanding and resilience, and enhanced appreciation for the instability and fragility that can result during and after a crisis. This new knowledge will come from schools and be enacted and embodied by the school leaders. A new leadership model will appreciate that knowledge will include educating the whole person (Elliott and Hollingsworth, 2020).

POST-NOTE

- This chapter raises the issue of mental health as a crucial component of leadership during and after any major crisis. How does this align with your perceptions about essential leadership priorities in a crisis?
- The pandemic highlighted inequities in schooling in Australia, which left many students disadvantaged by the closure of schools. What suggestions do you have in confronting and minimizing these inequities to avoid students falling further behind academically?
- This chapter presented the case of Australia in dealing with crisis. Compare and contrast the descriptions in this chapter with those experiences you have encountered in your part of the world.
- Compose a list of strategies to manage crises as discussed in this chapter. What other important and unique leadership characteristics or behaviors are necessary to effectively manage a crisis?

REFERENCES

Aguliera, E., and Nightengale-Lee, B. (2020). Emergency remote teaching across urban and rural contexts: Perspectives on educational equity. *Information and Learning Sciences, 121* (5/6), 471–78. https://www.emerald.com/insight/content/doi/10.1108/ILS-04-2020-0100/full/pdf?title=emergency-remote-teaching-across-urban-and-rural-contexts-perspectives-on-educational-equity.

Australian Institute for Teaching and School Leadership, (AITSL).

Bodenheimer, G., and Shuster, S. M. (2020). Emotional labour, teaching, and burnout: Investigating complex relationships, *Educational Research, 62*(1), 63–76. https://doi.org/10.1080/00131881.2019.1705868.

Bolman, L. G., and Deal, T. E. (2017). *Reframing organizations: Artistry, choice, and leadership* (6th ed.). Wiley.

Clarke, S. (2016). School leadership in turbulent times and the value of negative capability. *Professional Development in Education, 42*(1), 5–18. https://doi.org/10.1080/19415257.2015.1010692

Cloninger, K. (2018). Educating in a time of crisis: Why well-being is essential. *Curriculum and Teaching Dialogue, 2*(1 and 2), xii–xxiii.

Cohen, W. A. (2016). *Drucker on leadership: New lessons from the father of modern management.* Wiley.

Darling-Hammond, L. (2010). *The flat world and education: How America's commitment to equity will determine our future.* Teachers College Press.

Egan, K. (2008). *The future of education: Reimagining our schools from the ground up.* Yale University Press.

Elliott, K., and Hollingsworth, H. (2020). A case for reimagining school leadership development to enhance collective efficacy. *Australian Council for Educational Research.* https://doi.org/10.37517/XYQS1429.

Fullan, M. (1993). Why teachers must become change agents. *Educational leadership, 50*(6), 12–17.

Fullan, M. (2005). *Leadership and sustainability: System thinkers in action.* Corwin.

Gallant, A. (2013). Self-conscious emotion: How two teachers explore the emotional work of teaching. In M. Newberry, A. Gallant, and P. Riley (Eds.), *Emotion and school: Understanding how the hidden curriculum influences relationships, leadership, teaching, and learning* (pp. 163–81). Emerald Publishing Group.

Gallant, A., and Riley, P. (2013). The emotional labour of the aspirant leader: Traversing school politics. In M. Newberry, A. Gallant, and P. Riley (Eds.), *Emotion and school: Understanding how the hidden curriculum influences relationships, leadership, teaching, and learning* (pp. 81–97). Emerald Publishing Group.

George, M. J., Odgers, C. L., Piontak, J. R., and Russell, M. A. (2018). Concurrent and subsequent association between daily digital technology use and high-risk adolescents' mental health symptoms. *Child development, 89*(1). 78–88. https://doi.org/10.1111/cdev.12819.

Hargreaves, A. (1998). The emotional practice of teaching. *Teaching and Teacher Education, 14*(8), 835–54.

Hargreaves, A., and Fullan, M. (2012). *Professional capital: Transforming teaching in every school.* Teachers College Press.

Hargreaves, A., and Fullan, M. (2020). Professional capital after the pandemic: Revisiting and revising classic understandings of teachers' work. *Journal of Professional Capital and Community.* https://www.emerald.com/insight/content/doi/10.1108/JPCC-06-2020-0039/full/html.

Heifetz, R., Grashow, A., and Linsky, M. (2009). Leadership in a (permanent) crisis. *Harvard Business Review.* July–August. https://hbr.org/2009/07/leadership-in-a-permanent-crisis.

Jaroensutiyotin, J., Wang, Z., Ling, B., and Chen, Y. (2019). Change leadership and individual innovative behaviour in crisis contexts: An attentional perspective. *Social Behaviour and Personality: An International Journal, 47*(4). https://doi.org/10.2224/sbp.7773.

Kutcher, S., and Wei, Y. (2020). Mental health literacy: Past, present, and future. *The Canadian Journal of Psychiatry, 61*(3). 154–58. https://doi.org/10.1177/0706743715616609.

Noddings, N. (1992). *The challenge to care in schools.* Teachers College Press.

Parks, S., (2005). *Leadership can be taught: A bold approach for a complex world.* Harvard Business School Press.

Shaked, H. (2020). Social justice leadership, instructional leadership, and the goals of schooling. *International Journal of Educational Management, 34*(1), 81–95. https://doi.org/10.1108/IJEM-01-2019-0018.

Smith, L., and Riley, D. (2012). School leadership in times of crisis. *School Leadership and Management, 32*(1), 57–71. https://doi.org/10.1080/13632434.2011.614941.

Sonneman, J., and Goss, P. (2020). Covid catch-up: Helping disadvantaged students close the equity gap. *Grattan Institute Report.* https://grattan.edu.au/wp-content/uploads/2020/06/COVID-Catch-up-Grattan-School-Education-Report.pdf.

Topper, B., and Lagadec, P. (2013). Fractal crises: A new path for crisis theory and management. *Journal of Contingencies and Crisis Management, 21*(1). https://doi.org/10.1111/1468-5973.12008.

Tran, H., Hardie, S., and Cunningham, K. M. W. (2020). Leading with empathy and humanity: Why talent-centred education leadership is especially critical amidst the pandemic crisis. *ISEA, 48*(1). https://www.usccihe.org/tcelireading.

Chapter Three

The Challenge of Inequity in Educational Systems Under the Coronavirus Pandemic and Other Crises

Toward a New Model of Teacher Mentoring

Orly Shapira-Lishchinsky

PRE-FOCUS GUIDING QUESTIONS

- Can you brainstorm a few educational inequities, of any sort, that may result in schools when a severe crisis emerges?
- Can you suggest different ways of mentoring teachers to reduce educational inequity during the COVID-19 pandemic and other crises?
- How can we advance equity in leadership policies, proactively, to mitigate inequities during a school crisis?
- How does teacher mentoring occur in your school? Has the mentoring of teachers been disrupted during the COVID-19 crisis? If so, have any alternative approaches to mentoring been developed? If not, what would you do as the principal to continue teacher mentoring amid a crisis of the magnitude of COVID-19?

INTRODUCTION

As the world is grappling with the COVID-19 pandemic, more than 130 countries have closed schools nationwide, affecting nearly 80% of students globally (Gilbert et al., 2020). Decisions have led millions of students into temporary "home-schooling" situations (Karp and McGowan, 2020). The COVID-19 outbreak affects families, society, and economics (Fernandes, 2020). In an educational context, it is particularly damaging for economically or educationally disadvantaged students, who are placed at special risk.

The damage is expressed through learning difficulties, leading to an increased gap between disadvantaged students and those from more privileged backgrounds (Tabner, 2020). However, the COVID-19 outbreak also has prompted new examples of educational innovation, such as the use of mixed-media learning, video communications, and virtual classes (Guest et al., 2020).

While most studies have focused on students' difficulties during the COVID-19 pandemic (e.g., Tabner, 2020; also see chapter 9 in this volume), very few focus on teachers' inequity challenges derived from their interaction with their students (e.g., Guest et al., 2020). There are numerous examples of teachers' inequity challenges elicited from their work. The approach used to understand these challenges is derived from the socio-ecological model (Bronfenbrenner, 2005). Examples, among others, of some of the challenges faced by educators, include:

a. Students who do not have adequate resources for online learning as compared with other more advantaged students in the same class—an equity issue;
b. School principals who encourage online learning in elementary schools, however, are not aware of the fact that a high percentage of students do not have parents to support their learning at home during Zoom lessons (because, for instance, the parents are working)—a pedagogical and an equity issue;
c. School principals who are unaware of some important needed educational tools and resources students may need to support their learning—a pedagogical and an equity issue;
d. Teachers who have never had experience teaching online may suddenly be thrust into an online teaching environment amid a crisis—a pedagogical issue;
e. Parents of various socioeconomic situations who do not know how to support online learning in general—an equity issue; and
f. Policymakers who decided that only special-needs students will study in classes to reduce their learning gaps (while other students, with less-obvious learning difficulties, must study online, at home, despite the fact that they too might have special learning needs that must be met—an equity issue.

These aforementioned equity and pedagogical challenges become critical during a school crisis, especially when the crisis is of the magnitude of the COVID-19 pandemic. Therefore, it is crucial for extant and future mentoring programs to consider and deal with these extreme challenges to adequately prepare teachers. In this context, given the possibility of additional COVID-19 outbreaks or other crises in the future, the main objectives of this chapter are to suggest:

a. Different ways or forms of mentoring that help teachers come to grips with and possibly resolve critical issues of inequity in educational systems; and
b. A new model for teacher mentoring that may improve the capacity of teachers to deal with unusual situations when schools and teachers are thrust into crisis-mode.

Educators, in general, need to be cognizant of the fact that when schools confront severe crises that lead to the disruption of normal educational services, it is not unusual for normal routines to be disrupted as well. In this context, a school that, before the crisis, had a somewhat robust mentoring program might now experience a situation that would likely disrupt the continued mentoring of teachers. Such a gap might severely hamper a teacher's progress. New teachers, especially, might be disadvantaged; perhaps this too is an equity issue, albeit not the purpose of this chapter to discuss in depth. Without receiving the professional support teachers need, their success in the school might be in jeopardy.

THEORETICAL BACKGROUND

The Context: Inequity in Educational Systems

The terms equality and equity are often used interchangeably; however, they differ (Salazar et al., 2018). Equality is typically defined as treating everyone the same and giving everyone access to the same opportunities. Equity refers to proportional representation in those same opportunities. To achieve equity, leadership policies in educational systems may result in an unequal distribution of resources. Although unequal, this is considered equitable, because it is necessary to provide access to education for low-income students (Bogotch and Shields, 2014).

Inequity in educational systems often begins with pre-K education and continues in elementary, secondary, and high schools. Students from low-income homes are less likely to have access to prestigious schools and often have less-qualified teachers. This disparity continues throughout their educational experiences, with less access to top universities (Green, 2017). Additionally, teachers in schools with large populations of low-income students are often underqualified or less experienced (Arar, 2015). All these challenges result in obstacles for students. These disparities, amid a crisis, become even more extreme as we have seen in the COVID-19 pandemic. Thus, mentoring goals must reflect our desire for equity, rather than equality.

MENTORING AND THE SOCIO-ECOLOGICAL MODEL

People create contexts, and contexts create people (Cardno *and* Robson, 2016). Therefore, we cannot separate teachers from their social context during their mentoring. Therefore, the basis for fully understanding the varied needs of teachers is premised on the socio-ecological model (SEM) (Bronfenbrenner, 2005), which emphasizes various workplace (contextual) dimensions (figure 3.1).

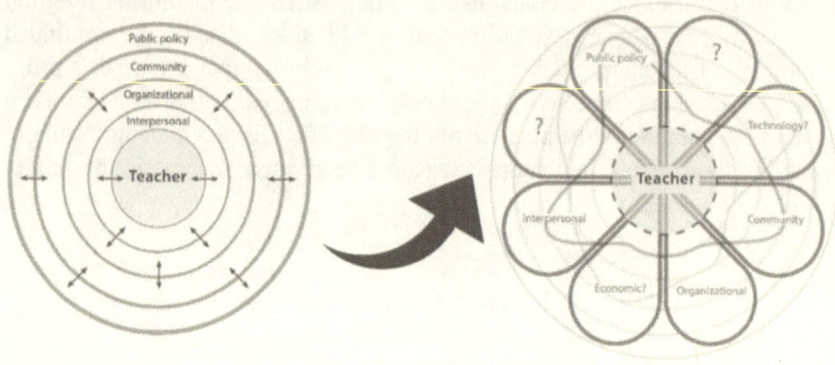

The original SEM   The new model

Figure 3.1. Toward teacher mentoring during the COVID-19 pandemic and other crises. *Source*: Bronfenbrenner, 2005

The original SEM focuses on the child's biological and psychological development (Bronfenbrenner, 1979). The SEM has been broadened to help understand the multifaceted and interactive effects of personal and environmental factors that determine behavior in various fields. Thus, researchers from different research areas, such as economics (e.g., Schlüter et al., 2017), public policy (e.g., Simplican et al., 2015), health education (Langille and Rodgers, 2010), and education (Xiao et al., 2019), elicit from Bronfenbrenner's (1979) original model a new model with new interpretations and definitions of the dimensions around the individual depending on the context.

In all these studies, the number of the model dimensions is equal to the layers in Bronfenbrenner's (1979) original model and the meaning of these dimensions (individual, interpersonal, organizational, community, and policy) correspond to the layers of the original model (individual, micro, meso, exo, and macro). However, the interpretation of each dimension changed based on the study context (e.g., education, public health system, public policy). Figure 3.1 illustrates these common dimensions.

This chapter suggests a new mentoring model, with all the known and unknown dimensions considered simultaneously, without a hierarchy between the factors. The structure of Bronfenbrenner's original model encourages us to consider one or two dimensions. The new model can simultaneously integrate the mentoring process from a variety of dimensions (e.g., community, policy, economics, and technology). Thus, this new model can fill the theoretical lacuna by dealing with inequity in education via the mentoring teachers.

The shortcomings of Bronfenbrenner's original model are reflected by several issues:

a. The model has been criticized for the difficulty in testing the theory empirically. The new model elicits new dimensions that may be incompatible with different inequity challenges, depending on the nature of the crisis.
b. The Bronfenbrenner model is limited to distinct socially organized dimensions, and within and between each dimension, there are bidirectional influences only.

Notwithstanding these limitations, the new model proposes the relevance of the present dimensions to the inequity context. This is especially important for grappling with a major school crisis. Additionally, the new model uncovers additional dimensions beyond the original factors presented in Bronfenbrenner's model. Moreover, eliciting unknown dimensions while evaluating existing ones may advance an interdisciplinary approach and encourage equity educational advances during various school crises by looking at the same phenomena from different viewpoints (e.g., economics or technology).

To summarize, this chapter proposes a new interdisciplinary model for mentoring during school crises, with all the emergent factors considered simultaneously in the same scenario, without a hierarchy of factors. The lines in the new model represent the level of the potential emergent dimensions of the new model.

MENTORING VIA SIMULATION: TOWARD EQUITABLE EDUCATION

During the COVID-19 outbreaks, teachers by and large did not possess sufficient pedagogical skills to deal with various and sometimes intractable equity challenges. Thus, teachers needed assistance to expand their abilities to handle these challenges. A mentoring program that relies on simulations can go a long way to providing teachers with appropriate skills to handle a variety of important issues (Gilbert et al., 2018).

Parenthetically, the importance of a mentoring program for teachers at all levels of experience is axiomatic (Daresh, 2014). The ideas advanced in this chapter that support and encourage mentoring are similar to practices in mentoring in normal times. However, the crucial difference is that at a time of crisis the issues discussed and the strategies used (e.g., critical incidents; see Shapira-Lischinsky, 2013) are more complex and urgent because of additional seemingly intractable complications, especially in crises like COVID-19 (e.g., fear from illness, economic stressors, loneliness, and uncertainty).

Simulations provide opportunities for participants to practice skills in a realistic, yet risk-free learning environment (Anderson and Lawton, 2009; Thornton et al., 2017). Team-based simulations provide teachers with real-life scenarios and offer real-time feedback concerning the actions they have taken to solve the problem of inequity in educational systems. Teachers will be able to see their peers' responses to different scenarios, thus enabling them to more effectively answer and solve equity problems and issues. Thus, these simulations have the power to track the teachers' knowledge and to change their modes of thinking, which, in turn, enables them to become better problem-solvers toward reducing inequity in education (Shapira-Lishchinsky, 2018).

In the context of the COVID-19 pandemic and other crises, simulations can lead to fruitful discourse, where the participants take part in roleplays in which the characters play the role of school principals, students, teachers, and parents in situations related to real-life school-inequity experiences.

This new theoretical model may support different styles of simulations:

a. *Lab simulations*, a relatively sterile environment (a room containing video equipment and a screen), that involves teachers from different schools, who engage in roleplaying with professional actors regarding inequity challenges in education.
b. *Simulations that are held inside the school* of the teachers. The participants are teachers from the same school, and these also feature roleplays with professional actors. In both types of simulations, the teachers have the opportunity to learn from peer feedback, as they are taking part in roleplay that mirrors the functions of decision-makers (Shapira-Lishchinsky, 2014). As a result, this experience allows these teachers to explore different approaches, test diverse strategies, and arrive at a better understanding of key real-world aspects of inequity in education relate to their school culture (Watts et al., 2018).

c. *Online simulations* enhance the learning process by creating a virtual reality (e.g., by Zoom) that challenges participants to solve problems in a complex and dynamic manner (Berends and Romme, 1999). Online simulations have been known to bring out participants' latent cognitive abilities through problem-solving. They also arouse a high level of thinking. Participants have an opportunity to return to the start of the simulation and learn new ways to respond to the challenge of inequity in education.

The learning that occurs in the different styles of simulations is an integral part of the systematic acquisition of concepts, knowledge, and skills that can result in improved equity in educational systems (Geithner and Menzel, 2016). Previous studies support using simulations to mentor teachers, since they sharpen complex decision-making processes, and foster higher-level thinking and reflections (Shapira-Lishchinsky, 2018). Thus, simulations, which deal with inequity challenges in educational systems may help teachers transfer their knowledge to real educational situations that they might encounter (Shapira-Lishchinsky, 2013).

To summarize, previous studies have described the nature of mentoring as a method of enhancing teachers' competence while dealing with inequity in education (Shapira-Lishchinsky, 2018). Effective mentoring in a variety of simulation styles can help teachers improve their communication skills and gain more confidence in their professional capability. Hence, the new theoretical model has the potential to promote equity in education via simulations of different patterns and styles and to provide a possible remedy to the shortcomings of mentoring programs during times of crisis (Storey and Cox, 2015).

THE SOCIO-ECOLOGICAL MODEL AND SIMULATION IN THE CONTEXT OF A SCHOOL CRISIS

Within the context of the socio-ecological model, simulations that include roleplaying may be based on various dimensions:

a. The *interpersonal* dimension refers to the relationship between the students and their teachers. The *challenge* may appear in cases in which part of the students opt to miss virtual meetings because of concentration problems. Therefore, the teachers would make an effort to develop teaching skills that may assist these students.
b. The *organizational* dimension refers to the relationship between the students and the school administration. The *challenge* may appear when the

students perceive an unsupportive environment that fails to offer them the required resources (e.g., school software), while the teachers try to find alternative technologies (e.g., free software) to support their learning.
c. The *community* dimension comprises, for example, interactions between students and their parents. The *challenge* may appear when parents cannot help their child's virtual learning, and the teachers try to find solutions to support those students' learning so that they are on equal footing with students who have parental support.
d. The *public policy* dimension refers to regulations that encourage or require social distancing. The *challenge* may appear when regulations cause students emotional distress (e.g., students who are afraid to use public transportation to get to school, while their families cannot afford private cars) and the teachers try to give emotional support to these students to help them function in these conditions.

Further, within the context of the model, there are stages of mentoring through different styles of simulations. They include:

Stage 1: Each teacher develops a scenario describing one or more challenges teachers face in the context of the particular crisis at hand based on real cases.
Stage 2: Simulation groups role-play the scenarios. The mentor asks volunteers to engage in the roleplay while the remaining teachers observe their peers. Afterward, the entire group debriefs by viewing the recorded simulations and discussing their observations.

Practical Implications and Guidelines

The new interdisciplinary mentoring model can have a strong practical impact in several ways on:

a. Educational leadership (e.g., designing effective simulation professional development programs dealing with inequity in any educational system);
b. Organizational learning (e.g., whether attending to and achieving equity in schools will increase student achievement across all diverse constituencies);
c. The mentoring curriculum itself (e.g., what specific content and activities need to be created to address inequities and improved teacher performance overall); and
d. Society (e.g., the degree to which teachers can improve equity education in their community via simulations and other proactive measures).

Here are some guidelines for teachers and school leaders to consider:

a. *Ensuring strong leadership from the top*—Principals and other leaders need to believe in the efficacy of mentoring, and they should monitor that it is not in any way compromised or curtailed in a crisis.
b. *Hiring or assigning highly qualified mentors*—Teacher mentors themselves need to display competencies to encourage the improvement of teaching. However, this is even more critical in a crisis that compromises equity issues in a school. These mentors must be committed to equity work and be able to address them proactively.
c. *Articulating a strategic approach to dealing with inequities during a crisis*—With a strategic plan in place, a school ensures that role expectations are clearly defined and that an emergency plan is ready at all times.
d. *Monitoring the program to ensure continuity*—The principal or delegate must monitor the efficiency and effectiveness of the mentoring program. Relatedly, programmatic assessment or evaluation needs to be established. Data need collection and analysis regularly.
e. *Remaining proactive*—Perhaps above all else, especially initially, a proactive leader (teacher or principal) must be cognizant of inequities and have on hand well-designed simulations that adequately address the needed issues in a given school during a particular crisis.

CONCLUSION

Most studies (e.g., Boekaerts, 2016) in the literature to date have focused on the mentoring process but not on its inequity dimensions. This chapter, in contrast, endorsed an interdisciplinary mentoring model via the use of simulations that emerged from the work and model proposed by Bronfenbrenner (2005). The proposed interdisciplinary model focuses on cases of inequity in educational systems. The model's interdisciplinary approach, integrating different disciplines (e.g., educational systems, mentoring, and equity), makes this model a unique platform for addressing and resolving inequities in schools during crises.

POST-NOTE

- What may constrain your school from effectively creating and sustaining a strong mentoring program? If your school has one in place, are equity issues addressed?

- Based on your experience, do educational leaders realize the importance of the use of simulations to reduce inequity in various educational systems?
- In my research, I found that simulation use has a positive impact on furthering the goals of mentoring, especially during crises. Does this align with your thinking and experience during COVID-19 and other crises?
- Near the end of the chapter, several practical suggestions were listed. React to them. What other practical suggestions can you offer to maintain a mentoring program to help teachers teach and, at the same time, address equity issues during periods of crisis?

REFERENCES

Anderson, P. H., and Lawton, L. (2009). Business simulations and cognitive learning: Developments, desires, and future directions. *Simulation and Gaming, 40*(2), 193–216. https://doi.org/10.1177/1046878108321624.

Arar, K. H. (2015). Leadership for equity and social justice in Arab and Jewish schools in Israel: Leadership trajectories and pedagogical praxis. *International Journal of Multicultural Education, 17*(1), 162–87. http://dx.doi.org/10.18251/ijme.v17i1.938.

Berends, P., and Romme, G. (1999). Simulation as a research tool in management studies. *European Management Journal, 17*(6), 576–83. https://doi.org/10.1016/S0263-2373(99)00048-1.

Boekaerts, M. (2016). Engagement as an inherent aspect of the learning process. *Learning and Instruction, 43*(1), 76–83. https://doi.org/10.1016/j.learninstruc.2016.02.001.

Bogotch, I., and Shields, C. M. (Eds.). (2014). *International handbook of educational leadership and social (in) justice (Vol. 29).* Springer.

Bronfenbrenner, U. (1979). *The ecology of human development.* Harvard University Press.

Bronfenbrenner, U. (Ed.). (2005). *Making human beings human: Bio-ecological perspectives on human development.* Sage.

Cardno, C., and Robson, J. (2016). Realizing the value of performance appraisal for middle leaders in New Zealand secondary schools. *Research in Educational Administration and Leadership, 1*(2), 229–54. https://files.eric.ed.gov/fulltext/EJ1207742.pdf.

Daresh, J. (2014). *Teachers mentoring teachers: A practical approach to helping new and experienced staff.* Corwin.

Fernandes, N. (2020). *Economic effects of Coronavirus outbreak (COVID-19) on the world economy.* http://baku8km.khazar.org/bitstream/20.500.12323/4496/1/Economic%20Effects%20of%20Coronavirus%20Outbreak.pdf.

Geithner, S. and Menzel, D. (2016). Effectiveness of learning through experience and reflection in a project management simulation. *Simulation and Gaming, 47*(2), 228–56. https://doi.org/10.1177/1046878115624312.

Gilbert, M., Pullano, G., Pinotti, F., Valdano, E., Poletto, C., Boëlle, P. Y., and Gutierrez, B. (2020). Preparedness and vulnerability of African countries against importations of COVID-19: A modeling study. *The Lancet*, *395*(10227), 871–77. https://doi.10.1016/S0140-6736(20)30411-6.

Gilbert, K. A., Voelkel Jr., R. H., and Johnson, C. W. (2018). Increasing self-efficacy through immersive simulations: Leading professional learning communities. *Journal of Leadership Education*, *17*(3), 154–74. https://journalofleadershiped.org/wp-content/uploads/2019/02/17_4_gilbert.pdf.

Green, T. L. (2017). Community-based equity audits: A practical approach for educational leaders to support equitable community-school improvements. *Educational Administration Quarterly*, *53*(1), 3–39. https://doi.org/10.1177/0013161X16672513.

Guest, J. L., del Rio, C., and Sanchez, T. (2020). The three steps needed to end the COVID-19 pandemic: Bold public health leadership, rapid innovations, and courageous political will. *JMIR Public health and surveillance*, *6*(2), 19043. https://publichealth.jmir.org/2020/2/e19043/.

Karp, P., and McGowan, M. (2020). 'Clear as mud': Schools ask for online learning help as Coronavirus policy confusion persists. *The Guardian*. https://www.theguardian.com/australia-news/2020/mar/24/clear-as-mud-schools-ask-for-online-learning-help-as-coronavirus-policy-confusion-persists.

Langille, J. L. D., and Rodgers, W. M. (2010). Exploring the influence of a social-ecological model on school-based physical activity. *Health Education and Behavior*, *37*(6), 879–94. https://doi.10.1177/1090198110367877.

Salazar, M. L., Cashman, E. M., and Eschenbach, E. A. (2018, October). Equality vs. equity: Using assets and cultivating students. In *2018 IEEE Frontiers in Education Conference (FIE)* (pp. 1–3).

Schlüter, M., Baeza, A., Dressler, G., Frank, K., Groeneveld, J., Jager, W., and Schwarz, N. (2017). A framework for mapping and comparing behavioral theories in models of socio-ecological systems. *Ecological Economics*, *131*, 21–35. https://doi.org/10.1016/j.ecolecon.2016.08.008.

Shapira-Lishchinsky, O. (2013). Team-based simulations: Learning ethical conduct in teacher trainee programs, *Teaching and Teacher Education*, *33*, 1–12. https://doi.org/10.1016/j.tate.2013.02.001.

Shapira-Lishchinsky, O. (2014). Toward developing authentic leadership: Team-Based Simulations, *Journal of School Leadership*, *24*(5), 979–1013. https://doi.org/10.1177/105268461402400506.

Shapira-Lishchinsky, O. (2018). *International aspects of organizational ethics in educational systems.* Emerald Publication, Howard House.

Simplican, S. C., Leader, G., Kosciulek, J., and Leahy, M. (2015). Defining the social inclusion of people with intellectual and developmental disabilities: An ecological model of social networks and community participation. *Research in Developmental Disabilities*, *38*, 18–29. https://doi.org/10.1016/j.ridd.2014.10.008.

Storey, V. J., and Cox, T. D. (2015). Utilizing TeachLivE™(TLE) to build educational leadership capacity: The development and application of virtual simulations. *Journal of Education and Human Development*, *4*(2), 41–49. http://jehdnet.com/journals/jehd/Vol_4_No_2_June_2015/5.pdf.

Tabner, I. T. (2020). *Five ways Coronavirus lockdowns increase inequality.* https://dspace.stir.ac.uk/retrieve/c3161b0f-8871-4807-8ac5-7d278368dfda/Tabner-Conversation-2020.pdf.

Thornton III, G. C., Mueller-Hanson, R. A., and Rupp, D. E. (2017). *Developing organizational simulations: A guide for practitioners, students, and researchers.* Taylor and Francis.

Watts, L. L., Ness, A. M., Steele, L. M., and Mumford, M. D. (2018). Learning from stories of leadership: How reading about personalized and socialized politicians' impacts performance on an ethical decision-making simulation. *The Leadership Quarterly, 29*(2), 276–94. https://doi.org/10.1016/j.leaqua.2017.04.004.

Xiao, H., Jingmin, L., and Kaixiang, W. (2019). *The influence of school curricular, environmental, and traffic intervention on the physical activity level of student groups based on a socio-ecological model* (No. 915). file:///C:/Users/user/Downloads/EasyChair-Preprint-915.pdf.

Chapter Four

A Swerve in Practice in Times of Crises

Rethinking Teacher Evaluation Anew

Helen M. Hazi

PRE-FOCUS GUIDING QUESTIONS

- How is teacher evaluation conducted in your school during "normal" times?
- During a school-related crisis you have experienced, has the nature or form of teacher evaluation changed in any way?
- What is it about a disaster that makes our search to get back to normalcy a double-edged sword?
- The author of this chapter takes two radical positions by arguing that the principal should not be expected to aim for normalcy in a time of crisis, nor continue to assume the burden of instructional improvement as an instructional leader. What is your position on one or both and why?

INTRODUCTION

A death, hurricane, flood, wildfire, and shooting require educators to pause from the day's routine. In these moments, educators can find opportunities to creatively deal with change and loss. I recall visiting a principal of a high school in a small rural community, when the death of two of his students in a car accident prompted him to schedule class visits to the funeral home and timeouts from the school day in the gym where teachers and students could find comfort in sharing their collective grief. The principal apologized for the disruption and not being able to see him in action!

We have not fully prepared our principals if we do not remind them of the uncertainties of practice that are beyond their control and encourage them to see the unexpected benefits of breaking with normalcy. The greatest barrier to judgment is uncertainty—"not the subjective uncertainty we feel when we exercise our judgment, but the uncertainty in the world to which our judgments apply" (Hammond, 2007, p. xi). The COVID-19 pandemic of 2020, and beyond, has reminded us quite dramatically that uncertainty does exist, if, indeed, we have somehow forgotten.

As schools reopen, educators have had to cope with a wide range of issues from cleaning and ventilation to liability should staff or students get sick (Weatherspoon and Fagenson, 2020). As principals learn to navigate a hybrid world, one where remote and in-school instruction coexist, principals are under stress to maintain normalcy as if possible and desirable. Yet, such thinking seems doomed to provoke even more stress and the quest for a new rubric to guide education through times of change and crisis (Schaffhauser, 2020). While uncertainty is a topic in teacher education, it is addressed for principals in limited places (e.g., in organizational decision-making and risk; see Hameriri et al., 2014).

In this chapter, I argue that the disruption of the pandemic gives educators an excuse to swerve from current practice. A swerve is a cultural shift in thinking that comes not as a dramatic revolution but in a small turn away from a path (Greenblatt, 2011). Such disruption could encourage educators to temporarily suspend practice to reimagine teacher evaluation as it could be. My argument rests on three claims: the uncertainty of teaching, the burden of instructional leadership, and the dysfunctional nature of teacher evaluation. Each is addressed separately in the following sections. Then, in the final section, I propose a way to reimagine teacher evaluation.

UNCERTAINTY IN TEACHING

Many educators seem to believe that teaching and learning are controllable. The often touted claim that teachers are the most influential in-school factor to student achievement continues even during the pandemic (see, e.g., ECS, 2020). However, a few scholars write about uncertainty in teaching but vary in how they approach and deal with it. Some, like Jackson (1986), who wrote about teaching and pedagogical uncertainty during the early accountability movement, recommended ways to reduce the uncertainty during teaching, such as with visual monitoring of faces and by asking students questions. Floden and Clark (1988), writing about an uncertain knowledge base, favored some amount of uncertainty since it led teachers to improve their practice.

Still, Heisling's (2007) critique of writings and research helps frame different dimensions to include origins of uncertainty, stances, and teacher responses. Teachers may deny uncertainty so that they avoid disclosing professional inadequacies—that they fall short of successful practice, stay in safe and oversimplified instructional routines, lower expectations for students, and are less likely to grow as teachers. School reform, another source of uncertainty, according to Heisling, may be counterproductive to the very change it hopes to promote. In such circumstances teachers can become angry and frustrated, blaming students for their failure to protect themselves, especially if teacher performance is less than adequate.

A time of crisis, such as disasters, creates uncertainty and stress in people and on the system. When schools closed in the early days of the pandemic in the U.S., instruction went online, and educators coped with new forms of communication and technology. Teachers and students experienced stress, anxiety, isolation, and depression. Schools faced technology challenges, truancy, and unequal access (Kurtz, 2020). Students with food insecurity, homelessness, insufficient internet, disabilities, and mental health needs, including abuse and neglect, were among those missing instruction (Makori and Dusseault, 2020; Spark, 2020).

At the start of the pandemic, some states were liberal in their thinking about evaluating instruction, with some waiving all teacher evaluation while others waived the use of student growth data. Still others warned that only a few rubric items applied to observe online learning and cautioned that not all students had internet access, but encouraged teacher feedback nonetheless (Will, 2020a). Teachers could use their score from the previous school year or before the shutdown, if not on an improvement plan. In some collective-bargaining states in the United States, teachers negotiated memoranda of understanding regarding work hours, meetings, and the amount of student contact (Sawchuk, 2020). Items specific to online teaching included submission of lesson plans, use of preclosure observations, VAM rating held harmless, and the deadline for evaluation (Hazi, 2020a).

Into the fall of the 2020–2021 school year, schools in some states faced shifts in enrollment, budget shortfalls and lack of resources, privacy concerns, teacher layoffs, and retirements. While planning for a hybrid of parent-preferred online and in-person schooling, school leaders in some districts began to shift to more face-to-face learning as infection rates declined. Teacher concerns turned to their safety, protective gear, and adapting instruction to minimize groups of students who varied per day for different blocks of time (Schwartz, 2020). While teacher evaluation is just beginning to be addressed in news sources (Will, 2020b),[1] teachers hoped to delay school openings with strikes and litigation (Walsh, 2020) for one-third of the 3.3 million teachers who are over fifty and potentially vulnerable to the virus. This portends to be an uncertain year, especially since teachers have been declared "critical essential workers" and could be exempt from isolation requirements (Smith,

2020). (See Hatch, 2020 for international news on school responses to COVID-19.) We should also pause to examine our expectations for principals.

RETHINKING PRINCIPAL AS INSTRUCTIONAL LEADER

Since the school effectiveness movement of the 1980s, there has been an unquestioned, seductive belief that principals can be instructional leaders. This has been a convenient policy tool of accountability,[2] despite limited evidence that teacher evaluation leads to instructional improvement of teachers (Donaldson, 2009). Yet we place principals in an untenable position, blaming them for something over which they have limited control, time, and expertise—the improvement of teachers.

Control. We take for granted that principals are supposed to improve teaching performance, which, in turn, is to improve student learning. This is a long-standing belief that principals and feedback drive this improvement. Educators have used their understandings about giving feedback to students and applied it to teachers. Teachers report that they find feedback from other teachers (86 percent) and mentors and coaches (82 percent) more useful than from principals (Prado et al., 2018). Oliveras-Ortiz (2017) found that teachers tend to have low trust levels of their administrators to lead their instructional coaching efforts. Teachers have reservations because administrators are seldom in classrooms, are unaware of what goes on in the classrooms daily, and lack content expertise to accurately provide feedback.

Time. Lavigne and Good's (2019, p. 138) review of time studies revealed that even though the federal initiative, "Race to the Top" required principals to spend more time in classrooms. Their increased time (from 2.4–2.5 percent to 9.26–17 percent) was relatively small compared to time spent in other duties. Principals typically report constraints on their ability to evaluate teachers: time (to evaluate and to improve), inability to watch typical instruction, observation instruments that are "too bulky, too cumbersome," and school culture and stress of employment decisions (Donaldson, 2011, p. 23).

Expertise. Some believe that if principals would just learn and use the teacher effectiveness research that they would have the expertise they need to improve teaching (Lavigne and Good, 2015, 2019). However, this belief assumes that this research is "generic" and fits all contexts (subjects, grades, student abilities, and lessons). This type of thinking omits the importance of content knowledge and context in instructional improvement.

Through interviews, Lochmiller (2019) found that teachers tend to trust principals who have their same content expertise when giving feedback. To improve instruction, Stein and Nelson (2003) theorize that principals need to know at least five different types of knowledge: content knowledge, content pedagogical knowledge, how students learn a subject matter, how teachers learn, and effective ways of teaching teachers both individually and in community. With this unreasonable burden, the principal also is the lead in a dysfunctional practice.

THE DYSFUNCTIONAL NATURE OF TEACHER EVALUATION

Enduring, as well as emerging, influences in its history have complicated the practice of teacher evaluation[3] and have confounded attempts to solve this especially "wicked" problem (Hazi, 2019). I have explicated this problem in the previously cited work, but, in short, the enduring influences include: its conflicting formative and summative purposes, and evaluation of the generic teacher with "the" objective instrument. Federal involvement in teacher evaluation starting with No Child Left Behind, which only further complicated what had become a dysfunctional practice. Emerging influences since 2000 include state oversight and involvement, metrics mania, and multiple measures. These influences and attempts to "fix" teacher quality, including the two decades of federal involvement in the United States, has led to what I call *a principal-centric approach* to teacher evaluation, that is, one where the principal or instrument is central to the process, rather than the teacher or his/her learning or improvement.

According to two policy "influentials," current teacher evaluation systems will *not* help teachers improve (e.g., Darling-Hammond, 2012) and are not fair, psychometrically valid, nor reliable for consequential employment decisions (Berliner, 2018). Darling-Hammond (2012) concludes that value-added is seriously flawed to evaluate individual teachers. She cites studies where student achievement did not improve or, in fact, dropped, where teachers collaborated less because they competed, and where major research organizations believe it should not be used to make high-stakes decisions about teachers. Darling-Hammond also argues that teacher ratings are unstable, reflecting more whom they teach such as high or low-performing students, rather than how well they teach.

Berliner (2018) further explains that the use of student test scores is not valid, since standardized tests used by the states were not designed for the purpose of teacher evaluation. Berliner also considers teacher behavior too unstable and infrequently measured for principal observation to be reliable, and high-quality teachers more difficult to judge. He considers the current system to be adequate to hold a conversation with a teacher, but not to make consequential employment decisions. Instead, Berliner argues for an evaluation system to assess whether teachers are fulfilling their duties to be identified as an adequate teacher. This approach seems appropriate in times of crisis, as well as a basic way to think about a complicated process, given Berliner and Darling-Hammond's criticisms. Berliner (2018) endorses Scriven's (1994) duty-based evaluation.

RETHINKING AND REIMAGINING PRACTICE

Teacher evaluation is a practice that most concerns many during a time of crisis. What better time to pause and rethink what both principals and teachers do. Teacher evaluation is a wicked problem that defies simple fixes. When we ask many principals to be instructional leaders we ask them to have time and expertise, and we assume they have control over improvement when, in reality, teachers do. Since teaching is a complex and uncertain practice, and disasters accentuate that uncertainty, such is the time to rethink what we do, especially teacher evaluation.

Scriven (1994) argues that duty-based is a defensible way to evaluate teachers and is consistent with many established principles of evaluation (Hazi, 2020c; Stufflebeam, 2013). A principal would determine whether a teacher performs essential duties such as planning a lesson, constructing tests, grading papers, explaining a difficult concept, and managing discipline. This list of duties (fifty-two versions) was developed over thirty years and reviewed by several thousand teachers and administrators in the United States and Australia. It is "the only legitimate basis for evaluation, until a better one emerges" (Scriven, 2015, p. 8). Therein, the principal decides whether a teacher is "satisfactory"[4] to continue employment or if the teacher requires dismissal or remediation. Scriven's duty-based approach allows the principal to provide oversight, that is, "control, watchful care" ("Oversight," 2019) to ensure teachers do no harm. Fulfilling his/her legal responsibility of personnel evaluation, the principal may, but is not expected to, carry the more complex and time-consuming burden of dismissal or improvement. This supports Scriven's (1994, 2015) principle that formative is separate from summative and that the same person was never meant to both evaluate and improve a teacher.

A duty-based approach is the minimum that should be reasonably done in times of crisis, since there are many tasks that disrupt and compete with practice. This also should be the minimum to be expected of most principals. In anticipation of disasters, teachers and administrators could negotiate duties on the list, and place it in memoranda of understanding. They could agree on the weighting and rating of the duties to be used during the crisis. If there is time to reimagine evaluation with duty-based evaluation as its basis, then teachers and administrators can meet to discuss other components of evaluation as time permits. These, I argue for and defend, using principles of evaluation in the following.

Once the principal's judgment is verified by another administrator, this then triggers the development of different cases, both requiring multiple sources of evidence. Evidence includes lesson plans, student work, results of testing, and lesson artifacts.[5] If the case is for dismissal, this process substantiates the causes and develops in-depth the reasons for dismissal. If remediation, this process further diagnoses the teacher's needs and develops a plan to address those needs. In both, administrators and teachers with content and pedagogical knowledge[6] become members of a team that then works the teacher's case with time, will, and expertise. Since each teacher's circumstance is unique, the team builds a unique case. The principal continues his/her oversight by participating and monitoring the work of the team, following the course of action. A team comes to a consensus, takes actions as required over time, and consults with an attorney, when appropriate, even in the event of another improvement plan.

The duration and activities of each vary, depending on the teacher, grade, subject, and students involved. In the case of remediation, the teacher must be willing to engage in further experiences to improve. Improvement, in general, is defined "as evidence of teacher learning that results in progress in knowledge, behavior, and thinking about the pedagogy, curriculum, students and their interactions" (Hazi, 2020b, p. 99). However, each situation will require its definition of improvement, customizing its definition, sources of evidence, and description of progress for each teacher.

Teachers not in need of dismissal or remediation who want to study their teaching can participate with a peer or administrator partner, or in a network within or outside of their school. The goal is to have insights about their teaching, which can evolve from the study of a lesson, a series of lessons, a unit, or a period of six to nine weeks within one or across multiple subjects (Stigler and Hiebert, 2016). Reflection is an important element of this study of teaching. This option can occur in groups, consistent with systems-thinking and networking with other teachers (Bryk, 2015; Hazi and Garman, 2018). Such participation can also be considered professional development that can provide teachers with a much-needed safe space to study their practice. Such group study takes instructional improvement out of the purview of an individual classroom, and out of a one-on-one relationship with an administrator. Similarly, a teacher should be able to engage in self-study, relying on evidence and artifacts of student learning and reflection.

In addition to lesson study and network improvement communities, Sullivan and Glanz (2000) offer alternative approaches that include mentoring, peer coaching, portfolios for differentiated supervision, peer assessment, and action research. These alternatives promote what I call a *teacher-centric view of instructional improvement*, that is, an approach that focuses on teaching and learning and that treats teachers as learners instead of objects of principal control (Hazi, 2018). The teacher controls his/her improvement, often dictated by changing circumstances of classroom routines, and requiring usable knowledge that is situated in the context of the lesson, the subject, and class of students who have varying abilities. Teaching is complex and far from generic.

CONCLUSION

Schools across the world have been given an unusual opportunity so they can swerve from "normal" practices to rethink what they do. Teacher evaluation is one of those dysfunctional practices that defies fixes in both satisfying laws and regulations yet allows teachers the safe space to grow. Systems tend to promote uniformity in the name of fairness rather than in the name of what will help teachers to learn and improve. For many decades we have promoted principals as instructional leaders without considering whether expectations are reasonable for both the principal and teacher. Principals can facilitate the ensuing work of others who have the desire and expertise to be involved in improvement in a *teacher-centric view*. Maybe uncertainty in times of crises can free us from conventions that stabilize us, yet inhibit our ability to innovate.

POST-NOTE

- Now that you've had the opportunity to review the author's arguments, what school practice(s) should be placed on pause or reimagined during a time of crisis, and why?
- We, in education, tend to think of medicine as certain. However, there are voids in medical knowledge (e.g., the dose of medicine required for an individual may be inexact). In medicine, there are three types of uncertainty: 1) incomplete or imperfect mastery of available knowledge, 2) voids in current medical knowledge (e.g., like COVID-19), and 3) difficulty in distinguishing between the two. How do/should we prepare administrators and teachers for uncertainty? How do we acknowledge an uncertain practice and still inspire public confidence?
- On a more basic level, assess the authors' suggestions (e.g., duty-based evaluation). What do you think of it? Would/could it work in your school? Why/why not?

- What practical strategies can you employ to support teacher growth during a crisis?

NOTES

1. At this writing, Will (2020b) reports that teachers are anxious in states where teacher evaluation continues as if it's a normal school year: "You shouldn't have to 'defend yourself and prove that you're an effective educator in a pandemic" (para 2). Teachers also say, "it's unfair to make potentially high-stakes job-performance decisions when they're navigating new technologies, adjusting to different methods of teaching and trying to reach students who might not have reliable internet access or stability at home" (para 3). Districts are changing their rubrics and weighting of data, using portfolios, and encouraging shorter but more frequent observations with targeted feedback (Will, 2020b).

2. Using 95,000 principals to improve schools was considered by some as a "cheap" "silver bullet" (Peck et al., 2013). Arne Duncan, then U.S. Secretary of Education, believed that, "If at the end of the day, our 95,000 schools each had a great principal, this thing [school improvement] would take care of itself" (Wallace Foundation, 2009).

3. I think of evaluation and supervision as similar, yet not identical, like fraternal twins. "Since they both require evidence, involve judgment and being in the classroom, they are forever entangled" (Hazi, 2012, p. 8), and in schooling of the early twentieth century, the functions were invested in separate individuals. Both principals and supervisors made classroom visits to inspect and help, respectively.

4. Scriven (2015) recommends "satisfactory" to mean a minimum level of competence, or acceptable or adequate.

5. Since the teacher does more than teach, outcomes alone cannot be used to evaluate teachers. Multiple methods and multiple sources of evidence should be used to evaluate (Scriven, 1994). This is another principle of evaluation.

6. Evaluation should be both generic and particularized to the content, context, and students (Scriven, 1994). This is another principle of evaluation.

REFERENCES

Berliner, D. (2018). Between Scylla and Charybdis: Reflections on and problems associated with the evaluation of teachers in an era of metrification. *Education Policy Analysis Archives, 26*(54), 1–24. https://epaa.asu.edu/ojs/article/view/3820.

Bryk, A. S. (2015). 2014 AERA Distinguished lecture: Accelerating how we learn to improve. *Education Researcher 44*(9), 467–77. https://doi.org/10.3102/0013189X15621543.

Darling-Hammond, L. (2012, March 5). Value-added evaluation hurts teaching. *Education Week.* https://www.edweek.org/ew/articles/2012/03/05/24darlinghammond_ep.h31.html.

Donaldson, M. L. (2009). So long, Lake Wobegon? Using teacher evaluation to raise teacher quality. *Center for American Progress*. https://www.americanprogress.org/issues/education-k-12/reports/2009/06/25/6243/so-long-lake-wobegon/.

Donaldson, M. L. (2011, February). Principals' approaches to developing teacher quality: Constraints and opportunities in hiring, assigning, evaluation, and developing teachers. *Center for American Progress*. https://www.americanprogress.org/issues/education-k-12/reports/2011/02/23/9161/principals-approaches-to-developing-teacher-quality/.

Education Commission of the States (ECS). (2020, September 17). Key issues: Teaching. Online Policy Reports. https://www.ecs.org/research-reports/key-issues/teaching/.

Floden, R., and Clark, C. (1988). Preparing teachers for uncertainty. *Teachers College Record*, 89(4), 504–24. http://citeseerx.ist.psu.edu/viewdoc/download?doi=10.1.1.567.3012andrep=rep1andtype=pdf.

Greenblatt, S. (2011). *The swerve: How the world became modern*. Norton and Co.

Hameriri, L., Nir, A., and Inbar, D. (2014). Confronting uncertainty and risk: The contribution of leadership to school outcomes. *Planning and Changing*, 45(1/2), 48–82. https://eric.ed.gov/?id=EJ1145638.

Hammond, K. (2007). *Beyond rationality: The search for wisdom in a troubled time*. Oxford University Press.

Hatch, T. (2020, September 16). What does it look like to go back to school? It's different all around the world. *International Education News*. https://internationalednews.com/2020/09/16/what-does-it-look-like-to-go-back-to-school-its-different-all-around-the-world/.

Hazi, H. M. (2012). *Expert judgment: A concept for teacher evaluation in a postmodern world.* A paper presented at the annual meeting of the American Educational Research Association, Vancouver, British Columbia.

Hazi, H. M. (2018, April). *Instructional improvement: Challenging taken-for-granted notions about this purpose of supervision.* A paper presented at the annual meeting of the American Educational Research Association, New York, NY.

Hazi, H. M. (2019). Coming to understand the wicked problem of teacher evaluation. In S. J. Zepeda, and J. Ponticell (Eds.), *Handbook of educational supervision* (pp. 183–208). Wiley Blackwell Publishing.

Hazi, H. M. (2020a, May 1). Analysis of Lee County Florida memoranda of understandings (mous) and communications to address 7 items found in other mous. Unpublished analysis in possession of author.

Hazi, H. M. (2020b). Instructional improvement: A modest essay. *Journal of Educational Supervision* 3(3), forthcoming.

Hazi, H. M. (2020c, October 9–10). *Returning to our roots: Basic principles of evaluation examined.* A paper presented to the annual meeting of the Council of Professors of Instructional Supervision, Indianapolis, IN.

Hazi, H. M., and Garman, N. B. (2018, October 12). *Complicating instructional improvement: Examining assumptions and discovering generative thinking in Carnegie Foundation's new reform agenda.* A paper presented at the annual conference of the Council of Professors of Instructional Supervision, Bangor, ME.

Heisling, D. (2007). Regarding uncertainty in teachers and teaching. *Teaching and Teacher Education, 23*, 1317–1333. https://doi.org/10.1016/j.tate.2006.06.007.

Jackson, P. (1986). *The practice of teaching.* Teachers College Press.

Kurtz, H. (2020, April 10). National survey tracks impact of coronavirus on schools: 10 key findings. *Education Week.* https://www.edweek.org/ew/articles/2020/04/10/national-survey-tracks-impact-of-coronavirus-on.html.

Lavigne, A. L., and Good, T. L. (2015). *Improving teaching through observation and feedback.* Routledge.

Lavigne, A. L., and Good, T. L. (2019). *Enhancing teacher education, development, and evaluation: Lessons learned from educational reform.* Routledge.

Lochmiller, C. R. (2019). Credibility in instructional supervision: Catalyst for differentiation. In M. L. Derrington and J. Brandon (Eds.), *Differentiated teacher evaluation and professional learning: Policies and practices for promoting career growth* (pp. 83–105). Palgrave Macmillan.

Makori, A., and Dusseault, B. (2020, August 17). Students experiencing homelessness are largely invisible in school reopening plans. Center for Reinventing Public Education's *The Lens.* https://www.crpe.org/thelens/students-experiencing-homelessness-are-largely-invisible-school-reopening-plans.

Oliveras-Ortiz, Y. (2017). School administrators as instructional coaches: Teachers' trust and perceptions of administrators' capacity. *School Leadership Review, 12*(1), 39–46. https://scholarworks.sfasu.edu/slr/vol12/iss1/6/?utm_source=scholarworks.sfasu.edu%2Fslr%2Fvol12%2Fiss1%2F6andutm_medium=PDFandutm_campaign=PDFCoverPages.

"Oversight." (2019). *The free dictionary.* https://www.thefreedictionary.com/oversight.

Peck, C., Reitzug, U. C., and West, D. L. (2013). Waiting for 'super-principal': Examining U.S. policymaker expectations for school principals, 2001-2011. *NCPEA Education Leadership Review, 14*(1), 58–68. https://eric.ed.gov/?id=EJ1105264.

Prado Tuma, A., Hamilton, L. S., and Tsai, T. (2018). *A nationwide look at teacher perceptions of evaluation systems: Findings from the American Teacher Panel.* RAND Corporation. http://www.rand.org/pubs/research_reports/RR2558.html.

Sawchuk, S. (2020, April 28). 7 big issues for unions and districts in remote teaching agreements. *Education Week.* https://www.edweek.org/ew/articles/2020/04/28/union-district-agreements-for-remote-teaching-7-big.html?cmp=eml-enl-eu-news2andM=59564350andU=andUUID=5db99379423bd8f2b72457b68b37431b.

Schaffhauser, D. (2020, August 20). Rubric helps districts identify areas of improvement for fall return. https://thejournal.com/articles/2020/08/31/rubric-helps-districts-identify-areas-of-improvement-for-fall-return.aspx.

Schwartz, S. (2020, August 5). Classroom routines must change. Here's what teaching looks like under COVID-19. *Education Week.* https://www.edweek.org/ew/articles/2020/08/06/classroom-routines-have-to-change-heres-what.html?cmp=eml-enl-eu-mostpopandM=59685020andU=andUUID=5db99379423bd8f2b72457b68b37431b.

Scriven, M. (1994). Duties of a teacher. *Journal of Personnel Evaluation in Education, 8*(2), 151–84. https://doi.org/10.1007/BF00972261.

Scriven, M. (2015, February 12). Duties of a teacher. http://michaelscriven.info/papersandpublications.html.

Smith, C. (2020, September 13). Teacher departures leave schools scrambling for substitutes. https://apnews.com/911a83b084ec23debadbd92bf559916d?utm_source=ECS+Subscribersandutm_campaign=724ce7bc85-ED_CLIPS_09_14_2020andutm_medium=emailandutm_term=0_1a2b00b930-724ce7bc85-63603423.

Sparks, S. (2020, September 2). What do schools need to be better after coronavirus? *Education Week*. https://blogs.edweek.org/edweek/inside-school-research/2020/09/what_do_schools_need_to_come_back_from_coronavirus.html.

Stein, M. K., and Nelson, B. S. (2003). Leadership content knowledge. *Educational Evaluation and Policy Analysis*, *25*(4), 423–48. https://doi.org/10.3102/01623737025004423.

Stigler, J. W., and Hiebert, J. (2016). Lesson study, improvement, and the importing of cultural routines. *ZDM Mathematics Education*, *48*, 581–87. https://doi.org/10.1007/s11858-016-0787-7.

Stufflebeam, D. (2013). My tribute to a trail blazer: Evaluation iconoclast—Professor Michael Scriven. *The future of evaluation in society: A tribute to Michael Scriven* (pp. 73–91). Charlotte, NC: Information Age Publishing, Inc.

Sullivan, S., and Glanz, J. (2000). Alternative approaches to supervision: Cases from the field. *Journal of Curriculum and Supervision*, *15*(3), 212–35.

Wallace Foundation. (2009, October 14). Comments of U.S. Secretary of Education Arne Duncan to the Wallace Foundation's national conference on education leadership. https://www.wallacefoundation.org/knowledge-center/pages/if-schools-had-a-great-principal-education-leadership-an-agenda-for-school-improvement.aspx.

Walsh, M. (2020, September 10). Schools losing out so far in court challenges to pandemic orders. *Education Week*. http://blogs.edweek.org/edweek/school_law/2020/09/courts_denying_relief_in_schoo.html?cmp=eml-enl-eu-news2andM=59679642andU=andUUID=5db99379423bd8f2b72457b68b37431b.

Weatherspoon, L., and Fagenson, Z. (2020, September 8). Teachers, parents, students scramble as U.S. schools reopen. https://www.edweek.org/ew/articles/2020/04/20/should-teachers-be-evaluated-during-coronavirus-school.html?cmp=eml-enl-eu-news1andM=59507678andU=andUUID=5db99379423bd8f2b72457b68b37431b.

Will, M. (2020a, April 20). Should teachers be evaluated during Coronavirus school shutdowns? *Education Week*. https://www.edweek.org/ew/articles/2020/04/20/should-teachers-be-evaluated-during-coronavirus-school.html?cmp=eml-enl-eu-news1andM=59507678andU=andUUID=5db99379423bd8f2b72457b68b37431b.

Will, M. (2020b, October 15). Yes, teachers are still being evaluated. Many say it's unfair. *Education Week*. https://www.edweek.org/ew/articles/2020/10/15/yes-teachers-are-still-being-evaluated-many.html?cmp=eml-enl-eu-news1andM=59728117andU=andUUID=5db99379423bd8f2b72457b68b37431b.

Chapter Five

Rethinking Character Education in the Era of Online Schooling in Crises

Shazia Rehman Khan

PRE-FOCUS GUIDING QUESTIONS

- What are the goals and challenges of character education in schools?
- How can we rethink character education and how can it be supported in times of crisis?
- What do theory and research have to say about the challenges and possibilities for teaching character education in an online environment?
- What are some practical strategies that school leaders and other educators can utilize to help teachers more effectively teach in a COVID-19 and post-COVID-19 era, or in any crisis for that matter?

INTRODUCTION

Character education, globally, has been an integral part of the educative process. Schools and educational institutions not only provide skills necessary to live life but also help shape a person's meaning of the world and the very meaning of a "good life." The goal of character education in schools is to instill certain cultural and societal qualities that help shape a students' character. The challenges and opportunities of character education in schools are manifold and not only limited to moral dilemmas of the real world but also involve the nature of crises and challenges faced by all people as they seek novel solutions.

Our world is rooted in change as we confront a plethora of ethical issues and moral dilemmas. One of the chief functions of school is to teach students to recognize these ethical conundrums and to provide them with requisite knowledge and skills to intelligently confront them. Educators are uniquely positioned to help students grapple with these ethical and moral issues that they will inevitably confront. The development of one's character is an important prerequisite that enables students to successfully manage these challenges.

Character education, in the curriculum, and other related learning resources are readily available in many schools. The teaching of character education, however, even in normal times, has come under criticism in recent years. A more egregious problem is that, sometimes, it even gets lost or sidelined, especially when other exigencies become manifest. For instance, in the almost global effort at standards-based education that emphasizes student achievement above almost everything else, character education curricula have been given less attention (Arriazu and Solari, 2015). Moreover, when a school or societal crisis appears, the emphasis on character education is lessened. School leaders have an important role to play in supporting the delivery of character education, especially in times of crisis.

This chapter, framed on the ideas of John Dewey (1893/1967) and Axel Honneth (2006), aims, first, to help educators rethink the teaching of ethics (for purposes here we are equating ethics and character even though there are distinctions), and second, relatedly and importantly, to provide a model in which the place of character education within the curriculum will not lose its status when crises, of any sort, become manifest. The chapter will demonstrate that the teaching of character development can be attended to even in an online environment, especially in a crisis. Moreover, teaching in times of crisis utilizing online technologies, for instance, may serve as an invaluable opportunity to advance the teaching of character education in schools. After reviewing some selected literature in the field, some practical suggestions or strategies will be discussed in helping school leaders and other educators effectively maintain a focus on character education pedagogy.

GOALS OF CHARACTER EDUCATION

"Character education is best understood as a subset of moral education, concerned with the cultivation of positive character traits called 'virtues'" (Arthur et al., 2016, p. 20). Character can be understood as "an individual's set of psychological characteristics that affect that person's ability and inclination to function morally" (Berkowitz, 2013, p. 48). The goal of character education is to develop good character traits in a person. For that to occur, an approach commonly used is to teach and develop good habits as early as possible. Throughout history, schools have been seen as a mobilizer of character education (Dishon, 2017). Children are thought to be easily "teachable," particularly when it comes to developing moral character, and school is seen as an optimal venue to achieve such a societal goal. Many countries worldwide commonly increase funding to schools to support the teaching of values and beliefs deemed valuable for a functioning society and citizenship (Watz, 2011).

Schools throughout the world have relied upon a virtue-based approach to character education. Virtue-based character education tries to instill qualities and dispositions through habit formation by exercising balance between extremes and aims at the development of practical wisdom (Hatchimonji et al., 2020). It does so by using both direct (use of codes, creeds, mottos) and indirect methods (use of stories and literature) (Arthur et al., 2014; McClellan, 1999). An important aspect of this approach is to realize that to become "virtuous" good actions are not enough, but one also needs to critically examine one's values and emotions. Thus, a curriculum may emphasize activities designed to explore societally acceptable values and behaviors (Hartman, 2013).

Although there are many variants regarding a virtue-based approach to ethics, there is an agreement on a few critical elements (Arthur et al., 2014) such as that moral virtues are teachable, measurable, contribute to individual and societal well-being, can be taught through role-modeling, are instrumental in academic gains, and empower students through democratic citizenship. Virtue-based approaches to character education, however, have come under fire in recent years (Kristjánsson, 2013b) due to their simplistic approaches to the development of character. Moreover, questions about the effectiveness of virtue-based character education have been prominent (Kristjánsson, 2013a). Therefore, extant research indicates that there is a need to rethink character education.

RETHINKING CHARACTER EDUCATION

Current thought into character education harkens back to John Dewey (1893/1967) in his classic article "Teaching Ethics in High School." Dewey criticized the way ethics was taught in schools. He affirmed that solely teaching morals through rules and codes was wrongheaded. He was against an approach that utilized almost exclusively a virtue-based approach.

According to Dewey (1916):

> Morals are as broad as acts which concern our relationships with others. And potentially this includes all our acts, even though their social bearing may not be thought of at the time of performance . . . Certain traits of character have such an obvious connection with our social relationships that we call them "moral" in an emphatic sense—truthfulness, honesty, chastity, amiability, etc. But this only means that they are, as compared with some other attitudes, central:—that they

carry other attitudes with them. They are moral in an emphatic sense not because they are isolated and exclusive, but because they are so intimately connected with thousands of other attitudes which we do not explicitly recognize—which perhaps we have not even names for. To call them virtues in their isolation is like taking the skeleton for the living body . . . Morals concern nothing less than the whole character, and the whole character is identical to the man in all his concrete make-up and manifestations. To possess virtue does not signify to have cultivated a few nameable and exclusive traits; it means to be fully and adequately what one is capable of becoming through associations with others in all the offices of life. (pp. 357–58)

Dewey correctly emphasized that if "conduct" means distinctive human behavior, then moral conduct is not over and above it. In a similar vein, moral theory is nothing else but the analysis of conduct. He challenged the virtue-ethics approach to education, as he did not see morality as something apart from being human. For him, all human knowledge, activity, character, and conduct was the subject of ethics and character education. "The moral and the social quality of conduct are, in the last analysis, identical with each other" (Dewey, 1916, p. 358).

The method Dewey criticized is still being used in many schools (particularly among high school–aged students and even older undergraduates), especially in my part of the world, as the primary method to character education. The current crisis provides us with the opportunity to rethink the traditional school structures for teaching character and to focus on the human conditions and relationships within which we find ourselves, that is, examining the web of relationships inherent in human interactions and recognizing the inherent values embedded in these relationships.

According to Honneth (2006), recognition means, "empathetic engagement in the world, arising from the experience of the world's significance and value . . . [which] is prior to our acts of detached cognition. A 'recognitional' stance, therefore, embodies our active and constant assessment of the value that persons and things have in themselves" (p. 111). Thus, "priority of recognition" means that recognition comes before cognition and that our psychological development is tied to our social interactions based on the inherent worth that people and things have in themselves (Bates, 2019).

Honneth (2006) elaborates that our "selves" are entangled in the "selves" of others and our identity is formed within the relationships with others. Thus, the "intersubjectivity of ourselves" should become our focus rather than relying on self as the foundation of our identity and definition. He distinctly defined three modes of recognition that are linked to the three ways of development: "emotional support," which leads to self-confidence; "social esteem," which leads to self-esteem; and "cognitive respect," which leads to self-respect. Self-confidence, self-esteem, and self-respect are thus acquired in the intersubjective relationships through recognition of and interaction with others. These different ways of development occur in what Honneth (1995) calls "communities of value" (p. 111).

Through Honneth's eyes, premised on Deweyian philosophy, character education that fits students into standardized virtues, devoid of situating them within the web of human relationships, robs them of developing themselves as thoughtful caring citizens who can genuinely develop self-confidence and self-esteem through meaningful engagement with others. The development of moral responsibility, that is the foundation of character education, is explained concisely by Honneth (1995):

> [A] violation of the intersubjective expectation to be recognized as a subject capable of forming moral judgement. [. . .] the experience of this type of disrespect typically brings with it a loss of self-respect, or the ability to relate to oneself as a legally equal interaction partner with all fellow humans. (Honneth, 1995, pp. 133–34)

A curriculum devoid of nurturing human relationships in which students are unable to see and discover themselves within the larger social context is unproductive, if not harmful. Character education must be premised on nurturing these relationships and providing students with meaningful and sustained opportunities to explore societally held beliefs and values in a critical fashion (Honneth, 1995).

In sum, the common approach to character education in schools via an emphasis on teaching predetermined virtues, although simple, and perhaps effective in creating habits, is largely ineffectual in terms of building a sense of community, of students seeing themselves as part of others, in an environment of mutuality and dependency. Dewey's, and especially Honneth's, ideas offer a unique and new way of teaching the value of others and can dramatically offer a more meaningful approach to the teaching of character education.

Thus far, I argued that although the teaching of character is critical, schools can do a better job. My experience in this most recent COVID-19 pandemic crisis has provided a unique opportunity to improve upon the teaching of character via an online platform that was mandated and necessary given the nature of the crisis. While this new approach can certainly be implemented in normal times, it was, in fact, this recent crisis that allowed me and others an opportunity to create new inroads into character education.

PUTTING THESE IDEAS INTO PRACTICE: THE ROLE OF THE PRINCIPAL AND SOME OF THE APPROACHES UTILIZED

When school leaders are inevitably confronted by crises, especially of the magnitude of the COVID-19 pandemic, information technology becomes an invaluable resource to navigate the educative process. Of course, depending on the nature of the crisis, other modalities may be equally effective. However, in this section, I am describing how the COVID-19 crisis propelled many educators, all over the world, to explore online learning and how it allowed them to creatively deal with persistent curricular issues (in my case, the teaching of character education).

Information technology has enabled us with an immense opportunity to carve new structures and spaces for student learning. The teaching of ethics in schools has taken a novel turn where character education cannot be physically interactive, nor directly observational. Yet the pandemic crisis has given us the impetus toward integrating technology to teach more effectively. We found that through the online environment we were able to build structures to support trust-building, self-determination, and a shifting focus toward an "ethics of recognition" as well as building community (Honneth, 2006).

One of the ways we were able to implement our ideas of character education in an online context was to focus on a hybrid between traditional pedagogy and heutagogy. Heutagogy, which is marked by self-directed learning and pedagogy, wherein the role of the teacher is facilitative, encouraging students to actively engage with one another. Innovations in information technology ably supported this approach toward learning by facilitating new and exciting ways for students to collaborate and build communities of learners and practice. Rather than utilizing prescribed, often prepackaged programs all too common in many character education settings, we set up an educational environment aimed to encourage reflection and dialogue among students (Blaschke and Hase, 2016; Kenyon and Hase, 2013).

My purpose here is not to describe all of the specific online technologies we utilized (although a few will be mentioned), but rather to focus on our general approach to teaching character development based on the ideas of Dewey and Honneth, described earlier. Also, I will not describe in detail the specific objectives and lesson plans integral to a character education curriculum. This chapter has a different focus, as noted above.

Parenthetically, however, and very important, is that crisis enabled us to break away from traditional structures and ways of teaching. I am not certain that we would have been able to do so easily without a crisis interfering with the normal operations of schooling. Also, some of our school leaders, especially principals, encouraged us to explore new ways of, in their words, "presenting and teaching knowledge and content." Although these administrators knew little of the specific approaches to the teaching of character and ethics, they gave us the freedom to explore and develop new ways of teaching. Perhaps that is the greatest contribution a school leader can make, especially in a crisis. That is, believe in your teachers and provide the material and emotional encouragement to teach well.

So, with the support and encouragement of selected school administrators, we developed a curriculum based on six design elements of the heutagogic approach: exploring, creating, collaborating, connecting, sharing, and reflecting. I will briefly chart here how each of the design elements of heutagogy was used with minimal direction and support by teachers within an online schooling environment to encourage students to actively form communities of learning and thereby come to deep understandings about the nature of character development (Blaschke and Hase, 2016).

Fundamental to the approach we used was providing students with the freedom and opportunity to explore multiple ways to learn new things with each other, from various sources of knowledge. Students were encouraged to participate in how and what they wanted to learn. They were able to build their designs and learning processes around certain themes that we provided relevant to character education (Hase, 2013; Kenyon and Hase, 2013). Given space limitations, I cannot explicate our entire curriculum and related activities, but allow me to provide a few examples.

Using applications such as Flipboard (www.flipboard.com) allowed students to organize their learning communities and related resources around mutual topics of interest. Students were encouraged to self-select learning groups, when appropriate. At other times, depending on the maturity level of the student, they were assigned to groups as long as the topic was of interest to them. To foster independence in learning, students were given access to different learning materials and modules and asked to problem-solve various scenarios, cases, or ethical dilemmas. Teachers oversaw the process, charting student progress in each module or community and offering encouragement and situational assistance. Learning analytics for concept mapping (https://www.readingrockets.org/strategies/concept_maps), for instance, helped us chart student progress. The teacher's role was nondidactic, thus encouraging student exploration. This approach to character education is reflected in the literature I described earlier and particularly helpful to build student self-respect and confidence.

We refrained from offering specific solutions to various case dilemmas students confronted. "So, what's the solution?" one student asked. Another asked, "What do you think?" Students were encouraged to answer their questions through discussion and, at times, even debate. Rather than simply stating a position, students had to provide a rationale for their decisions and answers. Students were encouraged to ask each other questions, rather than to accept a person's position at face value. For example, after a debate where students presented different points of view on a subject, they were asked why they thought that their classmates' conclusions or points of view were different from theirs. Students then posted their views on a threaded discussion. This enabled them to think deeply about alternative ways of viewing a dilemma or problem.

Students came to realize that people can have different points of view on any given subject. It helped build a more inclusive and respectful environment in the class. In support of this approach, we relied on Duckworth (2006), who elaborated on the epistemological framework of the "having of wonderful ideas." Under this framework, teachers encourage students to explore answers on their own and to find ways to get to these answers with the support of others in their community.

Further, we used a variety of tools, in some cases suggested by a school leader, such as popplet (https://www.popplet.com/) and bubbl.us (https://bubbl.us/). These tools and others encouraged collaboration as students learned from each other and learned to work with each other. For content learning, reciprocal teaching was employed. We facilitated the forming of small groups of students and breakout rooms (as in https://zoom.us). Two other tools used to build and nudge students toward collaborations were group awareness tools (GATs) (which facilitate monitoring and regulation of collaboration through visual mapping) and collaboration strips (which serve as an explicit guide to learners about how to collaborate) (for details, see Strauß and Rummel, 2020). Students were encouraged to share their knowledge and solutions through discussion boards and formal and informal presentations of their ideas. Some tools included PowerPoint presentations, audio clips, recorded video, Prezi presentations, mind maps, and so on.

Lastly, the exercise of reflection on what is learned and how it is learned became a weekly exercise. Students kept online reflective learning journals or diaries that helped them map their learning and development. Students were given a say on how they wanted to be evaluated. Encouraged were participative forms of evaluation like peer assessment and self-assessment, making space for students to learn from each other and through self-reflection (Dick, 2013). Teachers served as guides and provided formative feedback personalized to each student's needs.

One of the issues that I faced while using this approach is that students were usually hesitant about the discussion of taboo topics, especially in open discussions. Often, they would also self-censor themselves in self-assessments. Thus, a teacher needs to show her/his vulnerabilities to make students see that together they can carve a space to talk about these topics and to give emotional support to each other. The focus of an ethics class should not be to discipline students but to get them to talk, to bring out their true feelings and opinions so that they can honestly connect with others and a trustworthy relationship can be built in the class. "[B]asic self-confidence has less to do with a high estimation of one's abilities than with the underlying capacity to express needs and desires without fear of being abandoned as a result." (Honneth, 1995, p. xiii).

Interestingly, the issue described above was, in large measure, mitigated by the fact that instruction occurred online. Students reported that they were more comfortable discussing certain topics online than they would have been having been face-to-face in a classroom. Hence, another teaching advantage prompted by crisis presented itself.

Our experiences demonstrate that a healthy classroom environment in the teaching of character should be filled with respect for each other's opinions, genuine care for each other's learning and growth, and overall well-being. Character building can never be detached from the context in which children exercise their agency, and thus students themselves must freely choose to take this responsibility as well. Online learning during a period of crisis prompted us to take a new and innovative approach to teach this subject.

Principal leadership is key to allow teachers to creatively explore alternate ways of teaching. In our case, several principals and other school leaders encouraged us to try new ways for the teaching of character. The textbooks and prepackaged curricula available in our schools before the crisis were of little use in an online teaching environment. New, creative ways had to be explored and developed. Conversations with principals offered us an opportunity to experiment that might not have been otherwise possible without the crisis. Put simply and frankly, school leaders were busily attending to logistical and administrative exigencies to help manage the crisis. Thus, we were able to forge new ways of thinking about the subject we taught. The use of online technologies exclusively aided us in implementing our ideas to rethink the teaching of character development.

CONCLUSION

The goal of character education is to help children become better in reflective and critical thinking and to develop children as independent learners so that they will develop communal values based on a sense of respect for oneself and others. In this chapter, I discussed how crisis opportunities may present themselves as a way to break free of old structures and to build new ways of teaching, by providing the case of the teaching of character education. Crises alone do not guarantee success in teaching. Rather, it is innovative ideas culled from extant research, supported by visionary school leaders who see the opportunity for growth and learning when crises eventuate.

POST-NOTE

- Based on your experience, how is character education taught, and how effective is it, whether it be during a school crisis or otherwise? Is there a difference?
- In this chapter, I raised questions about traditional and current ways of teaching character development in schools, and how we can build on the idea of communities for learning among students. This approach doesn't mandate specific ethical values or ways of behaving. Rather, it is based on the idea that students, when given opportunities for reflection, will emerge with a healthier sense of the meaning of character and ethical behavior. To some, this may be reminiscent of Kohlberg's ideas of moral education. What do you think, and what do you think about this approach to character education? And, let's say you were the principal of the school in which I worked. And say, you differed with my approach because you favored the virtues-based approach. What would you say or do as a school principal?
- The main idea presented in this chapter revolves around the recognition of ourselves and others, and the intersubjective nature of our identity, which furthers our sense of ethics. Does this align with how you understand ethics?
- How many school leaders have you known that envision opportunities "for growth and learning when crises eventuate"? What makes some leaders see opportunity in crises?
- What are other, perhaps more specific ways, school leaders can manage a crisis to support teaching and learning in general?

REFERENCES

Arriazu, R., and Solari, M. (2015). The role of education in times of crisis: A critical analysis of the Europe 2020 Strategy. *KEDI Journal of Educational Policy, 12*(2). http://eng.kedi.re.kr.

Arthur, J., Harrison, T., Carr, D., Kristjansson, K., and Davison, I. (2014). *Knightly virtues: Enhancing virtue literacy through stories*. Jubilee Centre for Character and Virtues.

Bates, A. (2019). Character education and the 'priority of recognition.' *Cambridge Journal of Education, 49*(6), 695–710. https://doi.org/https://doi.org/10.1080/0305764X.2019.1590529.

Berkowitz, M. W. (2013). The science of character education. In W. Damon (Ed.), *Bringing in a new era in character education* (pp. 43–64). Hoover Institution Press.

Blaschke, L. M., and Hase, S. (2016). Heutagogy: A holistic framework for creating twenty-first-century self-determined learners. In B. Gros, L. Kinshuk, and M. Maina (Eds.), *The future of ubiquitous learning: Learning designs for emerging pedagogies* (pp. 25–40). Springer Berlin Heidelberg. https://doi.org/10.1007/978-3-662-47724-3_2.

Dewey, J. (1893/1967). *The early works, 1882–1898: 1895–1898. Early essays* (Vol. 5). Southern Illinois University Press.

Dewey, J. (1916). *Democracy and education*. Free Press, Macmillan.

Dick, B. (2013). *Crafting learner-centred processes using action research and action learning*. In S. Hase and C. Kenyon (Eds.), Self-determined learning: Heutagogy in action (pp. 39–53). Bloomsbury Publishing.

Dishon, G. (2017). Games of character: team sports, games, and character development in Victorian public schools, 1850–1900. *Paedagogica Historica, 53*(4), 364–80. https://doi.org/https://doi.org/10.1080/00309230.2016.1270339.

Duckworth, E. (2006). *The having of wonderful ideas and other essays on teaching and learning* (3rd ed.). Teachers College Press.

Hartman, E. (2013). *Virtue in business: Conversations with Aristotle*. Cambridge University Press.

Hase, S. (2013). Learner defined learning. In S. Hase and C. Kenyon (Eds.), *Self-determined learning: Heutagogy in action*. Bloomsbury Academic.

Hatchimonji, D. R., Linsky, A. C. V., Nayman, S. J., and Elias, M. J. (2020). Spiral model of phronesis development: Social-emotional and character development in low-resourced urban schools. *Journal of Moral Education, 49*(1), 129–42. https://doi.org/10.1080/03057240.2019.1626703.

Honneth, A. (1995). *The struggle for recognition: The moral grammar of social conflicts*. MIT Press.

Honneth, A. (2006). *Reification: A recognition-theoretical view* (0275–7656). Tanner Lectures on Human Values.

Kenyon, C., and Hase, S. (2013). Heutagogy fundamentals. In S. Hase and C. Kenyon (Eds.), *Self determined learning: Heutagogy in action*. Bloomsburg Publishers.

Kristjánsson, K. (2013a). Ten myths about character, virtue and virtue education–plus three well-founded misgivings. *British Journal of Educational Studies, 61*(3), 269–87.

Kristjánsson, K. (2013b). *Virtues and vices in positive psychology*. Cambridge University Press.

McClellan, B. E. (1999). *Moral education in America: Schools and the shaping of character from Colonial times to the present*. Teachers College Press.

Strauß, S., and Rummel, N. (2020). Promoting interaction in online distance education: designing, implementing and supporting collaborative learning. *Information and Learning Sciences, 121*(5), 251–60. https://doi.org/doi/10.1108/ILS-04-2020-0090.

Watz, M. (2011). An historical analysis of character education. *Journal of Inquiry and Action in Education, 4*(2), 3. https://digitalcommons.buffalostate.edu/jiae/vol4/iss2/3/.

Chapter Six

Instructional Leadership in Times of Crises and the Goal of Schooling

Haim Shaked

PRE-FOCUS GUIDING QUESTIONS

- Are principals who focus on instructional leadership fulfilling a primary goal of schooling?
- How does the relationship between instructional leadership and the goals of schooling influence the application of instructional leadership in normal times?
- How does the relationship between instructional leadership and the goals of schooling influence the application of instructional leadership in times of crisis?
- How do times of crisis affect principals' priorities?

INTRODUCTION

Researchers and practitioners alike have long asserted that school principals need to serve as instructional leaders in their schools (Hallinger and Wang, 2015; Kaparou and Bush, 2016). Instructional leadership may be briefly explained as the comprehensive and direct involvement of principals in promoting high-quality teaching and learning for all students (Glanz, 2005; Neumerski et al., 2018).

While principals, in the past, were primarily responsible for managerial and administrative tasks, such as maintaining student safety, enforcing school policies, and overseeing schedules, today's principals are required to engage regularly in curricular and instructional issues so that students achieve academic success (Hallinger, 2018a; Shaked, 2018, 2019).

Instructional leadership is related, most fundamentally, to the goals of schooling. Identifying the ultimate goal of schooling has broad implications, both theoretical and practical. However, it has hardly been investigated. Biesta (2009) pointed to "the remarkable absence in many contemporary discussions about education of explicit attention for what is educationally desirable. . . . There is very little explicit discussion, in other words, about what constitutes good education" (p. 36). In particular, the primary goal of schooling was hardly examined in direct relation to its conceptual implications for instructional leadership (Shaked, 2018).

This chapter claims that because of the connection between instructional leadership and the question of the primary purpose of schooling, the perceptions of principals regarding the latter inevitably influences their attitudes toward the former. Put differently, some principals continue to treat curriculum and instruction as issues of secondary importance because of their perception of the school's main task. The current chapter presents this argument in general, and in particular in the context of times of crisis.

FUNDAMENTALS, DIMENSIONS, AND CONTRIBUTIONS OF INSTRUCTIONAL LEADERSHIP

Research has no doubt: The quality of teaching is the most important school-related factor that influences student outcomes (Aaronson et al., 2007; Clotfelter et al., 2007). That is, academic results of students depend crucially on their teachers' effectiveness, more than many other school factors such as curricula or student grouping patterns (Hattie, 2009). Quality teaching, which is a prerequisite for improved academic outcomes, requires constant nurturing and accompaniment by the principal as an instructional leader (Blasé and Kirby, 2009; Stein and Coburn, 2008).

Reviewing extensive literature, Stronge, Richard, and Catano (2008) pointed to five core areas of instructional leadership, which principals use to meet their school goals:

- Building and maintaining a school vision that establishes clear learning goals and garners school-wide, and even community-wide, commitment to these goals
- Sharing leadership by empowering the expertise of teacher leaders to improve school effectiveness
- Leading a learning community that provides significant staff development
- Collecting data for use in instructional decision-making

- Monitoring and encouraging the implementation of curricula and quality teaching methods by spending time in classes

The framework of instructional leadership presented by Hallinger and Murphy (1985), which is the most widely used in research (Hallinger and Wang, 2015), consists of three dimensions that include ten functions:

- *Defining the school mission*—including two functions: framing the school's goals and communicating the school's goals. Principals are responsible for ensuring a clear mission, which focuses on all students' academic progress, and for disseminating this mission carefully to staff.
- *Managing the instructional program*—including three functions: supervising and evaluating instruction, coordinating curriculum, and monitoring student progress. This dimension focuses on the principals' role in coordinating and controlling the school academic program.
- *Developing a positive school learning climate*—including five functions: protecting instructional time, promoting professional development, maintaining high visibility, providing incentives for teachers, and providing incentives for learning.

According to Leithwood and Louis (2011), the conceptualization of instructional leadership should include a "set of responsibilities for principals that goes well beyond observing and intervening in classrooms—responsibilities touching on vision, organizational culture and the like" (p. 6). Therefore, they identified four core leadership practices:

- *Setting directions*—defining organizational purposes
- *Developing people*—expanding the capacities of organizational members to pursue these directions
- *Redesigning the organization*—modifying the organization to align with and support members' work
- *Managing instructional program*—improving teaching and curriculum

A large research base links instructional leadership to positive school outcomes, including improved teacher practices and higher student achievement, in a variety of organizational contexts (e.g., elementary, middle, and high schools; public, private, and public charter), spatial contexts (e.g., urban and suburban schools), and temporal contexts from 1980 through the present (e.g., Glanz, 2005; Glickman et al., 2014; Goddard et al., 2010; Jacobson, 2011; May and Supovitz, 2011; Quinn, 2002; Supovitz et al., 2010). The effect of instructional leadership on student outcomes was found to be three to four times greater than that of transformational leadership, with leaders inspiring, empowering, and stimulating teachers (Robinson et al., 2008).

These empirical links between the active involvement of principals in instruction, its high quality, and achievement of students have led to scholars' broadly voiced call for contemporary principals to see instructional leadership as their top priority (Blasé and Blasé, 2004; Louis et al., 2010; Murphy et al., 2016; Neumerski et al., 2018; Robinson et al., 2008). The demand from principals to assume central responsibility for instructional leadership has spread around the world (Kaparou and Bush, 2016; Shaked, 2018; Supovitz et al., 2010).

This chapter deals with instructional leadership in times of crisis. To this end, we should first understand the relationship between instructional leadership and the major purpose of schooling, a topic that has not been directly addressed in the literature. In other words, is a major emphasis on instructional leadership by principals in consonance with the primary goal of schooling, as perceived by educators in general? If it is, then does a commitment to instructional improvement remain a priority in times of crisis? If it is not, then how is the effort to improve instruction affected in crises? Over the following sections, these questions will be addressed.

INSTRUCTIONAL LEADERSHIP AND THE GOAL OF SCHOOLING

To explore schools' core responsibility, an initial discussion is needed concerning the gamut of functions that schools perform. Biesta (2009, 2014, 2016) identified three primary functions of schools: *qualification*, *socialization*, and *individuation*.

- *Qualification* refers to providing children with the knowledge, skills, and understanding that will enable them to perform a wide range of actions. This function of schools ranges from providing particular qualification (e.g., training students for a specific job) to much more general qualification (e.g., acquainting learners with Western culture).
- *Socialization* refers to the many ways in which, through education, students become members of and part of a particular social, cultural, and political "order." Sometimes this function is actively pursued by schools, for example, when it comes to conveying certain norms and values. However, even when *socialization* is not a stated goal, it remains a central implicit function, included in a "hidden" curriculum, referring to norms, values, and beliefs conveyed in schools without conscious intention (Jerald, 2006).

- *Individuation* refers to encouraging students to remain independent of social, cultural, and political arrangements. This function implies to students that they should not simply be a "specimen of a more encompassing order" (Biesta, 2009, p. 40). However, it is debatable as to whether all education contributes to such *individuation*.

Of these three school functions, which is the most important? What is the main goal of schooling? The public expects schools to perform *qualification*, *socialization*, and *individuation* simultaneously (Tichnor-Wagner and Socol, 2016). As Labaree (2010) said about the expectations of parents and community members: "We want schools to provide us with good citizens and productive workers; to give us an opportunity and reduce inequity; to improve our health, reduce crime, and protect the environment" (p. 1).

However, the contemporary era of measurement and accountability in education that has affected schools all over the world, is based on a belief that what matters most is academic results, that is, *qualification*. Today's education policies focus on student achievement as measured by test performance: "In the end, every element of an effective accountability system must be evaluated by one and only one criteria: Did it help students learn and achieve more than they might have without the system?" (Reeves, 2014, p. 1).

The fundamental assumptions of instructional leadership regarding the desired ultimate goal of schooling have not yet been discussed in the existing literature. However, this leadership approach seems to be based on the conceptual underpinning that the ultimate responsibility of schools is to ensure students' learning and academic success (*qualification*). Based on this basic assumption—that schools should first and foremost provide a wealth of knowledge and information, offering students a place to learn about new subjects and acquire learning skills—principals are expected to focus their efforts on leadership behaviors designed to improve teaching and learning through ongoing management of curricula and instruction. In this context, instructional leadership is consistent with the outcome-based accountability environment, which is also based on a belief that what matters most is academic outcomes (Baird et al., 2016; Engel and Frizzell, 2015; Reeves, 2014).

The connection between instructional leadership and the academic goal of schooling (*qualification*), is important for understanding the challenges of instructional leadership in times of crisis. But before we get into this topic, let's explain how this connection may sometimes serve as an inhibitor of instructional leadership. The next section will explain how.

INSTRUCTIONAL LEADERSHIP IN CONTEMPORARY PRACTICE

Although the importance of instructional leadership for student achievement and school improvement is clear, some principals apply it only partially. While many principals do enact instructional leadership, some others do not, spending only a small portion of their time on instructional issues (Goldring et al., 2015, 2019; Prytula et al., 2013).

Instructional leadership is extremely necessary for school effectiveness but at the same time can also be challenging. Three major inhibitors of instructional leadership have been identified in the research literature.

- First, some principals do not have enough time to be involved in instructional leadership (Goldring et al., 2015; Murphy et al, 2016), mainly because of ongoing structural constraints in their time that push them to deal with other issues like budget management, building operations, and student discipline (Camburn et al., 2010; Prytula et al., 2013). Because a lot of their time is spent on unplanned and crisis-oriented issues, principals' efforts to work on instructional issues are rarely realized during day-to-day school activities.
- Second, some principals do not have the knowledge needed to function as instructional leaders—they lack "instructional leadership content knowledge," which refers to how students learn specific subjects, which teaching methods are effective in which contexts, and so forth (Goldring et al., 2015; Stein and Nelson, 2003). "Without an understanding of the knowledge necessary for teachers to teach well . . . school leaders will be unable to perform essential school improvement functions such as monitoring instruction and supporting teacher development" (Spillane and Louis, 2002, p. 97).
- Third, deep-rooted organizational norms deter some principals from encroaching on the instructional territory of teachers and therefore give up their role as instructional leaders (Murphy et al., 2016, p. 462): "When school leaders 'left teaching,' they immediately set themselves up as something different from teachers and an occupation different from teaching. They were no longer teachers. They did not want to be teachers. They were not in the teaching business. . . . They were managers and administrators.

Shaked (2018, 2019) claimed that the inhibitors of instructional leadership include not only the constraints and abilities of school principals but also disagreements with the conceptual framework that underlying instructional leadership. He suggested that perceptual inhibitors of instructional leadership, which are based on the way principals think about the need for instructional leadership and its effects, played an especially important role.

Specifically, Shaked (2018, 2019) pointed to a significant possible explanation for why some principals were involved in instructional leadership only to a limited extent: their perceptions about the ultimate, primary goal of schools. His study suggested that some principals believed they should not be too focused on improving teaching and learning (instructional leadership), because ensuring students' learning and results (*qualification*) is not the most important thing a school is tasked to do. Instead, a school's main task is a nonacademic one, that is, to meet the emotional needs of the students, to support their social integration, and to impart moral values (*socialization*).

These principals ascribed primary importance to the school's role in developing students' emotional well-being, including their sense of belonging and safety, happiness in the present, and optimism regarding the future. Moreover, these principals often distinguished between "instruction" and "education," claiming that schools are indeed required to teach their students through academic instruction (i.e., qualification), but that their first and foremost goal should be to edify students by developing them morally and promoting their humanistic and adaptive character traits such as responsibility, self-control, integrity, decency, and good manners (i.e., socialization).

In particular, principals who emphasized the school's main task as nonacademic noted that a school is a mini-community reflecting the larger, more mature society. Therefore, these principals upheld that schools should give their students the social tools required to function within their society. For example, they stressed teaching students to navigate social interactions with peers from different backgrounds and helping them become productive community members who work not only toward their interests but also on behalf of public interests. More broadly, principals who espoused the school's chief nonacademic aim claimed that schools play a significant role in preparing students for their future participation in the democratic process, that is, in instilling loyalty to their homeland and increasing awareness concerning social justice.

Some principals find it difficult to identify with the premise that students' mastery over subject-matter academic achievements (*qualification*) should be the schools' ultimate goal. Instead, they pinpointed emotional, social, and value facets of schooling (*socialization*) as its main goal. The next section will argue that in times of crisis, like the coronavirus pandemic, this phenomenon is more common.

INSTRUCTIONAL LEADERSHIP IN TIMES OF CRISES

A study currently underway is examining how Israeli principals perceive their instructional leadership responsibility during the coronavirus pandemic.

Although I am citing this study I am not discussing it in detail. My purpose is to indicate that a fairly large number of principals believe that in times of crisis they should not focus too much on instructional leadership, because it primarily assists them in promoting academic goals while the nonacademic socializing goals are of greater importance during such times. While on ordinary days most principals align with the expectation that they will serve as instructional leaders, in times of widespread pandemic quite a few principals choose to give priority to the socialization aspect of schooling over the qualification aspect of schooling, leading to a decrease in their involvement in instructional leadership.

These findings illustrate how, in times of crisis, some principals seem to address an external policy through a buffering strategy rather than a bridging strategy (Kohansal, 2015; Paredes Scribner, 2013). The concept of buffering, rooted in organizational and institutional theory, refers to cases where school leaders respond to external influences and needs by trying to insulate themselves, whereas the concept of bridging refers to principals' attempts to tailor organizational activities according to external demands and expectations (Kim and Kim, 2016). Because of their belief about the goals of schooling in times of crisis, principals temporarily insulate themselves from the expectations to make instructional leadership a key role by maintaining their prioritization of school's nonacademic goals over academic goals.

More broadly, gaps in the implementation of the instructional leadership policy may be understood through the concept of street-level bureaucracy, which was first presented by Lipsky (1969). In the end, policy implementation comes down to the street-level bureaucrats. These street-level bureaucrats are civil servants who interact and communicate with the general public. Inasmuch as they are responsible for making decisions that are appropriate for clients and their situations, they also use their discretion. The use of discretion by street-level bureaucrats cannot be removed from everyday practice because of the complexity and uncertainty involved in human service work. Thus, policy implementation is not only a top-down process; in fact, street-level bureaucrats contribute to this process, leaving their "fingerprints" on policies received from above (Carrington, 2005; Hupe and Buffat, 2014; Lipski, 2010). Using a buffering strategy, principals' insulation from the instructional leadership policy in times of crisis may be seen as motivated by a moral dilemma between meeting system expectations and working for the well-being of their students (Wang, 2018). Faced with more and more dilemma situations, principals are becoming more creative in deciding what to endorse, what to block, and what to ignore in schools as they carry out their educational agenda (MacBeath et al., 2012).

To ensure that principals do not eschew their responsibility to foster instructional improvement, awareness is a needed initial step. Principals have to realize that instructional leadership is likely to be compromised in times of crisis. Moreover, they have to understand that despite the perceived conflict between instructional leadership and socialization as the primary goal of schooling, the two functions may not be mutually exclusive. Effective principals can attend to both, even though one is perceived as more critical. To enhance principals' utilization of bridging rather than buffering or insulating strategies, both present and future principals should receive professional legitimacy for engaging more actively in qualification-oriented instructional leadership while continuing to fulfill their preferred socialization- and individuation-oriented school functions.

POST-NOTE

- Based on your experience, do school leaders realize that emphasizing instructional improvement is closely aligned with the major goal of schooling?
- In my research, I found that principals examine the basic assumptions about the major goal of schooling through a wide range of perspectives: systemic, organizational, value-based, and moral. Does this align with your thinking and experience?
- My chapter emphasizes that in times of crisis, principals prioritize the school's nonacademic goals (socialization) over its academic goals (qualification) and therefore may sidestep instructional leadership. Is that your experience?
- Finally, I suggested, in closing, that principals need not eschew their responsibilities for instructional leadership in crises. Awareness, I emphasized, is key in keeping the "eye on the prize," so to speak. Another suggestion or guideline for maintaining the emphasis on instructional leadership might be to strategically plan before crises inevitably come our way. Perhaps delegating a teacher leader, or an assistant to maintain focus on it, while the principal and others attend to the managerial aspects that are required in a crisis. What other guidelines or suggestions might you proffer?

REFERENCES

Aaronson, D., Barrow, L., and Sander, W. (2007). Teachers and student achievement in the Chicago public high schools. *Journal of Labor Economics*, *25*(1), 95–135.

Baird, J. A., Johnson, S., Hopfenbeck, T. N., Isaacs, T., Sprague, T., Stobart, G., and Yu, G. (2016). On the supranational spell of PISA in policy. *Educational Research*, *58*(2), 121–38. https://doi.org/10.1080/00131881.2016.1165410.

Biesta, G. (2009). Good education in an age of measurement: On the need to reconnect with the question of purpose in education. *Educational Assessment, Evaluation, and Accountability*, *21*(1), 33–46. https://doi.org/10.1007/s11092-008-9064-9.

Biesta, G. (2014). Cultivating humanity or educating the human? Two options for education in the knowledge age. *Asia Pacific Education Review*, *15*(1), 13–19. https://doi.org/10.1007/s12564-013-9292-7.

Biesta, G. (2016). *Good education in an age of measurement: Ethics, politics, democracy*. Routledge.

Blasé, J., and Blasé, J. (2004). *Handbook of instructional leadership: How successful principals promote teaching and learning* (second edition). Corwin.

Blasé, J., and Kirby, P. (2009). *Bringing out the best in teachers: What effective principals do*. Corwin.

Camburn, E., Spillane, J., and Sebastian, J. (2010). Assessing the utility of a daily log for measuring principal leadership practice. *Educational Administration Quarterly*, *46*(5), 707–37. https://doi.org/10.1177/0013161X10377345.

Carrington, K. (2005). Is there a need for control? *Public Administration Quarterly*, *29*(1), 140–61.

Clotfelter, C., Ladd, H. F., and Vigdor, J. L. (2007). Teacher credentials and student achievement: Longitudinal analysis with student fixed effects. *Economics of Education Review*, *26*(6), 673–82. https://doi.org/10.1016/j.econedurev.2007.10.002.

Engel, L. C., and Frizzell, M. O. (2015). Competitive comparison and PISA bragging rights: Sub-national uses of the OECD's PISA in Canada and the USA. *Discourse: Studies in the Cultural Politics of Education*, *36*(5), 665–82. https://doi.org/10.1080/01596306.2015.1017446.

Glanz, J. (2005). *What every principal should know about instructional leadership*. Corwin.

Glickman, C. D., Gordon, S. P., and Ross-Gordon, J. M. (2014). *Supervision and instructional leadership: A developmental approach* (ninth edition). Pearson.

Goddard, Y. L., Neumerski, C. M., Goddard, R. D., Salloum, S. J., and Berebitsky, D. (2010). A multilevel exploratory study of the relationship between teachers' perceptions of principals' instructional support and group norms for instruction in elementary schools. *The Elementary School Journal*, *111*(2), 336–57. https://doi.org/10.1086/656303.

Goldring, E., Grissom, J. A., Neumerski, C. M., Murphy, J., Blissett, R., and Porter, A. (2015). *Making time for instructional leadership*. http://www.wallacefoundation.org/knowledge-center/Pages/Making-Time-for-Instructional-Leadership.aspx.

Goldring, E., Grissom, J., Neumerski, C. M., Blissett, R., Murphy, J., and Porter, A. (2019). Increasing principals' time on instructional leadership: Exploring the SAM® process. *Journal of Educational Administration*, *58*(1), 19–37. https://doi.org/10.1108/JEA-07-2018-0131.

Hallinger, P. (2018a). Principal instructional leadership: From prescription to theory to practice. In G. E. Hall, L. F. Quinn, and D. M. Gollnick (Eds.), *The Wiley handbook of teaching and learning* (pp. 505–28). Wiley Blackwell.

Hallinger, P. (2018b). Bringing context out of the shadows of leadership. *Educational Management Administration and Leadership*, *46*(1), 5–24. https://doi.org/10.1177/1741143216670652.

Hallinger, P., and Murphy, J. (1985). Assessing the instructional management behavior of principals. *The Elementary School Journal*, *86*(2), 217–47. https://doi.org/10.1086/461445.

Hallinger, P., and Wang, W. C. (2015). *Assessing instructional leadership with the Principal Instructional Management Rating Scale*. Springer.

Hattie, J. (2009). *Visible learning: A synthesis of over 800 meta-analyses relating to achievement*. Routledge.

Hupe, P., and Buffat, A. (2014). A public service gap: Capturing contexts in a comparative approach of street-level bureaucracy. *Public Management Review*, *16*(4), 548–69. https://doi.org/10.1080/14719037.2013.854401.

Jacobson, S. (2011). Leadership effects on student achievement and sustained school success. *International Journal of Educational Management*, *25*(1), 33–44. https://doi.org/10.1108/09513541111100107.

Kaparou, M., and Bush, T. (2016). Instructional leadership in Greek and English outstanding schools. *International Journal of Educational Management*, *30*(6), 894–912. https://doi.org/10.1108/IJEM-03-2015-0025.

Kim, S., and Kim J. N. (2016). Bridge or buffer: Two ideas of effective corporate governance and public engagement. *Journal of Public Affairs*, *16*(2), 118–27. https://doi.org/10.1002/pa.1555.

Kohansal, R. (2015). Public school principals: Agents of bridging and buffering. *Journal of School Leadership*, *25*(4), 621–58. https://doi.org/10.1177/105268461502500403.

Labaree, D. F. (2010). *Someone has to fail: The zero-sum game of public schooling*. Harvard University.

Leithwood, K., and Louis, K. S. (2011). *Linking leadership to student learning*. John Wiley and Sons.

Lipski, M. (2010). *Street-level bureaucracy: Dilemmas of the individual in public service* (thirtieth annual edition). Russell Sage Foundation.

Lipsky, M. (1969). *Toward a theory of street-level bureaucracy* (IRP Discussion Papers No. 48–69). Institute for Research on Poverty (IRP), University of Wisconsin.

Louis, K. S., Dretzke, B., and Wahlstrom, K. (2010). How does leadership affect student achievement? Results from a national US survey. *School Effectiveness and School Improvement*, *21*(3), 315–36. https://doi.org/10.1080/09243453.2010.486586.

MacBeath, J., O'Brien, J., and Gronn, P. (2012). Drowning or waving? Coping strategies among Scottish head teachers. *School Leadership and Management*, *32*(5), 421–37. https://doi.org/10.1080/13632434.2012.739870.

May, H., and Supovitz, J. A. (2011). The scope of principal efforts to improve instruction. *Educational Administration Quarterly*, *47*(2), 332–52. https://doi.org/10.1177/0013161X10383411.

Murphy, J., Neumerski, C. M., Goldring, E., Grissom, J., and Porter, A. (2016). Bottling fog? The quest for instructional management. *Cambridge Journal of Education*, *46*(4), 455–71. https://doi.org/10.1080/0305764X.2015.1064096.

Neumerski, C. M., Grissom, J. A., Goldring, E., Rubin, M., Cannata, M., Schuermann, P., and Drake, T. A. (2018). Restructuring instructional leadership: How multiple-measure teacher evaluation systems are redefining the role of the school principal. *The Elementary School Journal*, *119*(2), 270–97. https://doi.org/10.1086/700597.

Paredes Scribner, S. M. (2013). Beyond bridging and buffering: Cases of leadership perspective and practice at the nexus of school-community relations. *Journal of Cases in Educational Leadership*, *16*(3), 3–6. https://doi.org/10.1177/1555458913498475.

Prytula, M., Noonan, B., and Hellsten, L. (2013). Toward instructional leadership: Principals' perceptions of large-scale assessment in schools. *Canadian Journal of Educational Administration and Policy*, *140*, 1–30.

Quinn, D. M. (2002). The impact of principal leadership behaviors on instructional practice and student engagement. *Journal of Educational Administration*, *40*(5), 447–67. https://doi.org/10.1108/09578230210440294.

Reeves, D. B. (2014). *Accountability in action* (second edition). Houghton Mifflin Harcourt.

Robinson, V. M. J., Lloyd, C., and Rowe, K. (2008). The impact of leadership on student outcomes: An analysis of the differential effects of leadership types. *Educational Administration Quarterly*, *44*(5), 564–88. https://doi.org/10.1177/0013161X08321509.

Shaked, H. (2018). Why principals sidestep instructional leadership: The disregarded question of schools' primary objective. *Journal of School Leadership*, *28*(4), 517–38. https://doi.org/10.1177/105268461802800404.

Shaked, H. (2019). Perceptual inhibitors of instructional leadership in Israeli principals. *School Leadership and Management*, *39*(5), 519–36. https://doi.org/10.1080/13632434.2019.1574734.

Spillane, J. P., and Louis, K. S. (2002). School improvement process and practices: Professional learning for building instructional capacity. In J. Murphy (Ed.), *The educational leadership challenge: Redefining leadership for the 21st century* (pp. 83–104). University of Chicago.

Stein, M. K., and Coburn, C. E. (2008). Architectures for learning: A comparative analysis of two urban school districts. *American Journal of Education*, *114*(4), 583–626. https://doi.org/10.1086/589315.

Stein, M. K., and Nelson, B. S. (2003). Leadership content knowledge. *Educational evaluation and policy analysis*, *25*(4), 423–48. https://doi.org/10.3102/01623737025004423.

Stronge, J. H., Richard, H. B., and Catano, N. (2008). *Qualities of effective principals*. Association for Supervision and Curriculum Development.

Supovitz, J., Sirinides, P., and May, H. (2010). How principals and peers influence teaching and learning. *Educational Administration Quarterly*, *46*(1), 31–56. https://doi.org/10.1177/1094670509353043.

Tichnor-Wagner, A., and Socol, A. R. (2016). The presidential platform on twenty-first century education goals. *Education Policy Analysis Archives*, *24*(64), 1–30. https://doi.org/10.14507/epaa.24.2224.

Wang, F. (2018). Leadership as a subversive activity: Principals' perceptions. *International Journal of Leadership in Education*, *21*(5), 531–44. https://doi.org/10.1080/13603124.2016.1259507.

Chapter Seven

Crisis Leadership

Principals' Resilience Under Extraordinary Pressure

Mary Lynne Derrington and Sonya Hayes

PRE-FOCUS GUIDING QUESTIONS

- In what ways might principal leadership in a crisis be different than in daily school leadership?
- What is the ongoing role of a principal's communication, networking, and professional development in preparedness for crisis leadership?
- What are the key leadership lessons from The National Preparedness Leadership Initiative (NPLI) framework that can be implemented and practiced daily?
- The theme of emotional intelligence and resilience during a crisis runs throughout the references presented in this chapter. Can these personal characteristics be taught and learned in a leadership preparation program?

INTRODUCTION

Crucial changes in the context of principals' work make the job more challenging than ever (Fullan, 2014). Principals have faced an unprecedented amount of crises in the past twenty years. A review of *Education Week* headlines reveals 385 mentions of crisis in the last two decades; consequently, schools and school districts are not assured of success in a continuously changing and uncertain educational world (Smylie, 2016). In times of crisis, change is required faster than educators can keep pace. The list of issues and questions that surface in a crisis can be overwhelming and range from deeply rooted issues such as inequities, to operational issues such as how to distribute supplies when the school is closed.

COVID-19 is the most recent phenomenon to affect schools and is added to a growing list of crises that principals face including school shootings, lead in water, social justice unrest, bomb threats, teacher strikes, and natural weather disasters. Unfortunately, the COVID-19 pandemic is not likely to be the last contemporary crisis that plagues principals. According to futurists, it is likely that periods of calm will continue to be interrupted by crisis and the most improbable events will happen regularly (Crews, 2020).

Turnover in principalship was already a challenge prior to the COVID-19 crisis, with nearly one in five secondary principals planning to leave the profession (Maxwell and Superville, 2020). A survey conducted by the National Association of Secondary Principals (NASSP) revealed that 45 percent of the principals responding during the 2020 crisis were considering leaving the job sooner than they had previous planned. The reasons for the turnover vary, but concerns with health, extreme pressure or stress, and lack of support are at the top the list.

Although a significant number of principals are prompted to leave the profession in a crisis, it is important to understand why many others are not deterred from their chosen profession. Many principals have found ways to manage the pressures and added stress in extreme and changing circumstances. Although 45 percent of the principals in the NASSP survey indicated the COVID-19 crisis has influenced their decision to leave the profession, 46 percent of the respondents indicated they were more committed to their schools and communities. This result indicates that many principals have found ways to handle the pressure of leading during the COVID-19 pandemic, and by exploring the crisis leadership experiences of principals across the United States we hope to offer a means to support principals in times of great uncertainty.

Through this chapter, we address the challenges that principals face in times of crisis and analyze their leadership responses. The data used in the analysis were obtained from a larger U.S. dataset of qualitative interviews, conducted through the Consortium for Policy Research in Education, of 120 principals from multiple school levels (elementary, middle, and high) in thirty-three different states in varying school contexts (urban, suburban, and rural). A research team, comprised of educational researchers from multiple states (including the second author of the current chapter), interviewed these principals on their leadership experiences during the initial months of schools closing due to the COVID-19 pandemic. We randomly selected fifteen transcripts from this dataset from different regions of the United States to explore how school principals responded during the COVID-19 crisis. We then used the three dimensions identified in the *National Preparedness Leadership Initiative (NPLI)* developed by Marcus, McNulty, Henderson, and Dorn (2019) at Harvard University, to explore meta-leadership as an effective framework for identifying a constructive view of school leadership under circumstances of extreme pressure and stress.

NATIONAL PREPAREDNESS LEADERSHIP INITIATIVE (NPLI) FRAMEWORK

The three dimensions of the NPLI framework are built on the concept of meta-leadership, meaning how a leader looks at problems, opportunities, and solutions from a meta perspective, defined as a larger context or the big picture. Specifically, through principal responses to a national study, we examine meta-leadership as viewed through the following three dimensions:

1. The *person* or personal characteristics of principals who exhibit emotional intelligence and who develop credibility and trusting relationships
2. The *situation* and a principal's grasp of the complex problem and actions taken through communication and decision-making
3. The *connectivity* and how principals build networks through partnerships, collaboration, and work with stakeholders

The focus of the chapter is a theory to practice perspective. The three dimensions are examined through examples of principal practice that demonstrate the principal as a meta-leader in a crisis. Moreover, the meta-leader analysis indicates that the three dimensions must be developed over time and practiced daily, not simply when a crisis occurs.

THE PERSON: PRINCIPAL AND PERSONAL ATTRIBUTES

Martin Luther King stated, "The ultimate measure of a man is not where he stands in moments of comfort, but where he stands at times of challenge and controversy." A leader's response during a time of crisis is a true measure of his attributes and character. Crisis leadership often refers to the capability of a person to lead under extreme pressure and develop a mindset of reflecting, adapting, and learning from a crisis and its aftermath (Gigliotti, 2016). Some school principals have faced crises such as school shootings, natural weather disasters, social upheavals, or the untimely death of a student or teacher, but every principal in the United States faced an unprecedented crisis when school buildings closed in spring 2020 due to the COVID-19 pandemic. The measure of these principals and their response to this crisis is exemplified through their attributes and character.

Leadership attributes are often discussed in theories about traits, skills, and behaviors. Leadership traits theory implies that a leader must possess various innate personal characteristics to be effective (Zaccaro, 2007). Skills theory, however, implies that a leader can develop leadership skills through professional learning (Mumford et al., 2000). In essence, skills are attributes gained from education, practice, and experience. Kapucu and Ustun (2018) developed a conceptual model that explains the leadership attributes that are most effective during a crisis. These personal attributes include decisiveness, flexibility, and communication, and the behaviors needed include problem-solving, team building, networking, and strategic planning. A leader does not need to innately possess these personal attributes and behaviors, but a leader can develop and hone them with practice and time.

The Meta-Leader

Marcus et al. (2019) refers to a leader in a crisis as a meta-leader. A meta-leader is a role model who remains level headed and calm during moments of crises and "possesses a depth of emotional intelligence" (p. 106). Emotional intelligence is defined through Goleman's (2011) framework as a leader who exhibits five key attributes:

1. *Self-awareness*: the leader's understanding of self and what drives them. Self-aware leaders understand both their strengths and weaknesses.
2. *Self-regulation*: the leader's ability to control their moods, impulses, and interactions with others. Leaders who self-regulate can control their emotions and remain calm and level-headed.
3. *Motivation*: the leader's understanding of what drives them and moves them forward. Leaders who possess strong motivation can inspire and motivate others.
4. *Empathy*: the leader's ability to understand others and their needs. An empathetic leader seeks to understand others and appreciate their experiences and views.
5. *Social Skills*: the leader's ability to work with others and get along well with others. A leader who possesses strong social skills can make connections with people from various backgrounds and cultures.

Many of the principals interviewed during the COVID-19 pandemic exhibited high emotional intelligence. Most of the principals were unaware that decisions were being made to close the school buildings, and many thought that the buildings would close for a few weeks and reopen. When they learned that the buildings would remain closed for the remainder of the school year, principals were determined to remain calm and keep the school community connected. They used words and phrases such as "cheerleader," "a calming presence," "hopeful and optimistic," "constantly connecting with others," and "pastoral" to describe their role during the crisis. One principal reflecting on his ability to lead during the COVID-19 crisis stated,

> I think that I've learned about my flexibility. Even though I work in a school that is very structured, I think that this gave us an opportunity to release ourselves from that Type A personality and to be risk-takers in ways that I think were very advantageous for our school community.

Another added, "I learned a lot about my ability for adaptive leadership. I think that the relationships that I had prior to this, I was able to lean into. I think that people knowing that you care about them does volumes for their well-being and for the work." As leaders during a crisis, principals need to be flexible and adaptable (Goleman et al., 2002), offer encouragement (Kouzes and Posner, 2007), and maintain connections and communications with others (Kapuccu and Ustun, 2018).

Servant Leadership

The principals in the COVID-19 leadership study exhibited high emotional intelligence, and they considered themselves to be servant leaders. As defined by Greenleaf (2002), "a servant-leader is servant first. It begins with the natural feeling that one wants to serve. Then conscious choice brings one to aspire to lead" (p.27). Spears (2010) listed ten characteristics of servant leadership that include: *listening, empathy, healing, awareness, persuasion, conceptualization, foresight, stewardship, a commitment to the growth of people*, and *building community*. Many of the principals in the study mentioned that they became principals because "they felt called upon to serve," or they wanted "to help others" and this need to serve was "amplified during the crisis." A principal in New York exemplified servant leadership when she stated,

> Throughout the whole process our philosophy was "do no harm." The decisions that we make, the supports that we provide, they need to benefit students and support students. Now is not the time to draw a line in the sand or to get overly stringent with something. It's about supporting kids. If a kid needs something, we're going to find a way to get it for that kid.

Burkett and Hayes (2018) used the term "apostle leadership" (p. 118) to describe the servant-leadership style of principals in Texas and their response to anti-immigration policies that were creating crises in schools that predominantly served Hispanic students. Students and parents in these schools were engulfed in a culture of fear and uncertainty due to immigration raids and confinement to detention camps. The principals in these Texas schools not only had a servant-leadership mindset, but they exhibited characteristics of *humility, integrity, compassion, fearlessness, ardor*, and *diligence* by advocating for undocumented students and families. The principals in the COVID-19 study shared similar apostolic traits of humility, integrity, compassion, fearlessness, ardor, and diligence as they advocated for their school communities to provide resources and maintain some semblance of school for their students.

Caretaker Leadership

Gigliotti (2016) found in his study on higher-education leaders and their response during crises that leaders are *comforters, caretakers, an institutional voice*, and a *"man of steel"* (pp. 191–93). Gigliotti maintained that "the primary goal of each crisis response remains the same—to maintain order, provide clarity, and restore confidence" (p. 198). As caretakers, principals lead with their heart, and they are committed to the communities that they serve (Rodriguez et al., 2009). The participants in the COVID-19 study established themselves as caretakers of the school community by clarifying information as quickly as possible, and remaining a constant and calming presence within the community.

Principals quickly established themselves as the caretakers during the COVID-19 crisis, and they mentioned the socioemotional well-being of their faculty as their number one priority. As one principal from Colorado explained, "I've been working a lot with my staff and ensuring their mental health and social-emotional well-being . . . that's top priority." Principals felt responsible for monitoring and supporting the mental health of teachers, particularly teachers who were socially isolated, who were responsible for supervising their own kids in remote learning, and who were expressing concern about their students' needs during the pandemic.

Many of the principals also discussed their teachers' concerns over the virus and the caretaker role principals assumed to help their teachers. A principal in Texas explained, "My teachers were struggling with a generalized fear of the virus and its impact on themselves, their friends and families, and the school community. It was my job to assuage those fears." Another principal from New York spoke of the "many layers of mental health" that needed to be addressed, and how as a caretaker, "It was my job to find support for my teachers, parents, and students."

Principals felt a sense of responsibility to be a caretaker because they did indeed carry the burden of caring for teachers and ensuring their mental health and well-being. As the architects of school culture, principals are asked to support teachers' well-being during normal school operations (Glanz, 2006), but this support was amplified during the COVID-19 crisis. Since teachers, students, and parents were overwhelmed, it was important for principals to be role models and to remain calm and consistent during the disruption.

Although the characteristics of the meta-leader developed from crisis leadership, a meta-leader exhibits these characteristics in everyday routines (Marcus et al., 2019). Based on the data from the COVID-19 leadership study, the principals who describe themselves as servant leaders and school caretakers appear to have led their school communities well during the initial months of the COVID-19 crisis. Being a servant leader with high emotional intelligence and serving as an advocate for all stakeholders is imperative to responding well during a crisis; however, this type of leadership is required of principals in their daily work as a school leader. Fundamentally, being an effective leader in the day-to-day operations of the school is a precursor to being an effective leader during a crisis. Principals, who develop their emotional intelligence and servant-leader attributes in their daily routines, will ultimately be a meta-leader in a moment of crisis.

THE SITUATION: PRINCIPALS' PERCEPTIONS AND ACTIONS

The personal attributes of principals in crisis are a strong indicator to how a principal perceives a crisis and responds. Leaders face various situations every day, and they must assess and understand the situation, predict how it will unfold, make a decision, and take action (Marcus et al., 2019). In times of crisis, timing is critical, and the leader must assess the situation quickly and take appropriate action. As crisis leaders, the principals in the COVID-19 study responded to their students and communities with advocacy and compassion when the school buildings closed. They advocated for technology and broadband resources so students could continue to learn; they maintained strong relationships with the community by providing support to families with food and resources, and they became the haven for their communities through virtual check-ins with students and helping families stay connected to the school community.

Advocates for Resources

One of the inequities that were exemplified during the pandemic was the lack of resources needed for students to continue learning at home. Schneider (2017) highlights the inequities that plague public schools:

> The resources are now differentially available to students. Unlike their high-poverty peers, children from middle-class and affluent households almost all have high-speed internet access at home, as well as web-enabled devices. They've got enough books to see them through the end of the crisis—twice as many, on average, as low-income families and African American families. Their homes are more likely to be set up in a manner that supports school learning. (p. 18)

Children who live in impoverished areas or rural areas lack technology resources such as computers and internet access. Principals across the United States spoke of the challenges of providing virtual learning for all students. A principal in Florida explained that he had many homeless students who lived in shelters without computers or the internet, and another principal in Tennessee spoke of her rural community and how there was limited internet access.

In response, principals worked with community leaders to "negotiate cheap internet or provide free internet." Principals also found ways to provide free computers for children. For principals in rural areas without internet access, they created home lesson packets for students and delivered them to students. Principals not only advocated for technology resources for students but they also found ways to provide food for students on free-and-reduced lunch. Many of the principals discussed coordinating with the district to provide groceries or meals for families and create food distribution centers.

Support for Families and Students

Numerous principals suggested that the socialization aspect of a school is equally as important as the academic aspect because children learn how to develop socially through interactions with other children. A principal from Minnesota explained, "Kids want to be together. Younger children learn how to get along with one another through touch and play—It is an important thing for their social development." Another principal from Connecticut added, "Kids need one-to-one support, motivation, and encouragement, but if they are in a virtual environment, they don't have the emotional support they need." Because schools are a salient avenue through which social and emotional competence among children and adolescents is developed (Collie, 2020), principals worried that children being physically isolated from one another would cause anxiety and stress.

In response, principals in the COVID-19 leadership study took the lead to reduce student isolation as much as possible by establishing virtual schools and engaging students in "fun and play." Other principals found ways to make home visits and stand on the curb to talk to children and parents. A principal in California created parent packets complete with social-emotional resources to support their children, and a principal in Georgia created a virtual network for parents to have "virtual playdates for their [elementary-aged] kids."

As community leaders, principals place a high value on getting to know each child individually and on establishing and maintaining interpersonal communications with parents (Rodriguez et al., 2009). In discussing his reactions to supporting families during the COVID-19 pandemic, a principal in Texas commented, "As a principal, you are hardwired to care. I think [in a crisis] it's kind of hard to worry about anything other than the people in your charge. You have to look at the emergency and assess what people need and then react." Another principal in California commented, "I think things that the kids and parents were struggling with was the fear of thinking that I'm not enough. I'm not good enough or smart enough to move onto the next level." Principals addressed the fears of parents and students by maintaining connections with parents and students and creating systems of support.

CONNECTIVITY: PRINCIPALS' CONNECTIONS TO STAKEHOLDERS

Principals facilitate the work of *all* stakeholders to ensure a united effort, and, as a result, even under times of duress, they provide students with needed knowledge and skills. To facilitate the unification of all stakeholders requires coherence, or unity of purpose with everyone striving toward the same goals (Zepeda, Derrington, and Lanoue, 2020). Coherence is also a way to assist others to make sense of what is occurring and how their work connects to the larger system. It is the coherence or the connections and relationships among people and the flow of information that makes it possible to coordinate activities and develop a common understanding of what to do and why it is important (Hatch, 2015).

Principals in times of crisis focus on maintaining a strong connection with their communities with relevant and timely communication. When asked if communication strategies changed during the COVID-19 crisis, a California principal responded, "I wouldn't say it's a big change. We had to double up communications a bit." While communication is important during a crisis, effective principals have established communication procedures well in advance so principals can stay connected with their stakeholders seamlessly.

The importance, and simultaneously the difficulty, of connecting with all stakeholders should not be minimized. A principal reflecting on the difficulty of bringing all stakeholders together to focus on commonalities under times of duress commented, "I think that's the hard part to do. When everyone is running on adrenaline and in crisis, it's difficult to look beyond what's your emergency at the moment." A crisis requires that a principal connects with entrenched organizational silos and get everyone on the same proverbial page.

While principals are skilled in leading staff, meta-leadership requires that a principal lead *up*, *down*, and *across*. In leading upward, principals must consider how to influence their supervisors, take steps to keep them informed about school issues and advocate for their school. Leading down involves stakeholders over whom the principal has direct authority such as teachers and other school personnel and students. Leading across requires principals to connect with those that they have no formal authority over such as parents, other educational entities such as the state department, and governmental agencies including law enforcement.

Leading Up: Connecting with Supervisors

Leading up is the process of communicating to those higher in the organizational hierarchy (Waldron 1999). Principals understand what is happening at their school and how staff, students, and families are experiencing a crisis. They are obligated to assist the superintendent or state department in doing what is best for young people and the community served by the school. There are several considerations when communicating to a supervisor especially during a crisis: the message content, the delivery style, and the personal reputation that has been developed with supervisors.

Messages are used to influence supervisors to employ effective logic and reasoning to persuade. Besides, messages that show benefits to the organization are preferred by supervisors than those that promote self-interests. Considered together, both the content of the message and the delivery style of the communicator is important in creating a positive impression. The impression and personal reputation earned by the principal over time promote credibility, whereas an aggressive communication style can be perceived by the supervisor as lacking competence and promotes a low opinion of the principal (Foste and Botero, 2012).

In a time of crisis, decisions at the top might be quickly made without full consideration of the impact on staff, students, and the community. Effective meta-leaders take appropriate action. For example, a New York principal described a district policy promulgated during the fast-paced decision-making period of the COVID-19 crisis that could have resulted in a negative impact on a religious holiday. Rather than merely complying, the principal took action. He reported, "I wrote an email to the chancellor describing how [the decision] was disrespectful to not just teachers, but to families and to kids and to everyone." Speaking up to the boss is not easy, but it is necessary.

During times of crisis a principal might have to exert influence beyond the school district, as this principal who advocated for a reconsideration of testing under the COVID-19 crisis did: "I sent a tweet to our commissioner of education challenging him to reconsider the testing piece." The principal continued, "The department of education, wherever you are, is messy and you have to be persistent." Likely principals have not given much thought to leading up and the importance of developing a mutually beneficial relationship with the state department and the superintendent or immediate supervisor. However, the more the supervisor understands the school's challenges and goals, the more likely it is that the principal will be supported.

Principals might be uncomfortable or perhaps ever fearful to confront their supervisor. The chain of command promotes obedience and compliance to those in authority (Marcus et al., 2019). The key is finding ways to constructively connect over time, not just under a crisis. Marcus et al. (2019) identified key positive behaviors for influencing the boss including: a) developing a positive relationship, b) diplomacy, and c) supporting the broader purposes of the organization. Principals who build a strong working relationship and develop trust with their supervisor will ultimately be able to communicate and connect effectively with them during a crisis.

Leading Down: Connecting with Stakeholders inside the School

Leading down in a school context is a principal's connectivity with stakeholders within the school, namely teachers and students. Marcus et al. (2019) explains that meta-leaders focus on building connectivity within the organization so that all members of the organization will work together in a time of crisis. Principals who create collaborative environments with transparency and trust set a positive tone for their schools and how internal stakeholders will respond in a crisis.

Connecting with Teachers and Staff

Principals work with their staff daily to establish a foundation of a shared purpose and unified mission. A principal in the COVID-19 study noted,

> First and foremost, if your people are really centered on the moral purpose of teaching and learning, they get themselves together. The determination and the ability to overcome the obstacles and the unknown, really it was remarkable the

tenacity that the staff had. And so when they're in it for children, they will do what it takes.

Principals across the United States echoed that when a principal takes the time to build a shared mission that focuses on the well-being of students, then their staff will respond with that same purpose during times of crisis. However, one principal added a warning that overconfidence regarding a principal's knowledge of their staff might be a detriment,

> Don't be so comfortable that you think you know your staff too well because they still have things you don't know about them. I've come to learn certain things in the big scheme of things about them and to really have empathy.

Another principal added, "I think that everyone to a varying degree had personal issues that they were dealing with [in the crisis]." Principals should recognize that in times of crisis, relationships might be strained and more difficult to navigate than normal. It is important to stay calm and focused as this California principal related following a recent crisis,

> People were edgy, all the different personality types emerged. You had the people that thought, "Oh, it's going to be fine in a week. No problem." You had the people who thought the sky was falling right away. It just was interesting to see the varied reactions that people had. You could tell everybody's personality just really came out. Move forward with caution, but still move forward.

As crisis leaders, principals must address their teachers' well-being and stress levels. Many teachers during a time of crisis need additional support from their principal. In the COVID-19 study, a principal from Florida discussed his teachers' need for connection and how he addressed it:

> They need to have the connection, and they need to see each other. So I created systems for teachers to connect through virtual team meetings and virtual professional development. Nobody stops our show. I know that my staff needs each other—it's right for teachers to connect with each other, or just to work on things online. And I just kind of made it happen.

By identifying the needs of their teachers, effective leaders find ways to connect with their staff and address those needs.

Effective principals also recognize the stress of their teachers and take action to address their well-being to maintain a connection with them. In the COVID-19 study, principals addressed the well-being of their staff in two primary ways: individual outreach and community building. Individual outreach included calling teachers at home to check in with them and ask them questions like "What did you do for yourself today?" and "What are you going to do so you're not on the computer for 14 hours?" A principal in New York mentioned that she sent gifts to teachers' homes to show appreciation for their hard work and stress.

To build community, some of the principals used morning Zoom meetings to support teachers by creating an open forum for raising concerns and providing an opportunity to process their feelings. Many principals mentioned that they felt the need to create space for laughter and fun to help ease staff stress. Some principals even hosted "happy hours" to provide space for staff to socialize and spend time together. A principal from Georgia discussed the actions she took to care for her staff:

> During our weekly check-in meetings, it's really mostly just checking in on them and seeing how they're doing. We have a little giggle together. For Teacher Appreciation Week, I collected pictures of all of them, and I created a video and it was to that new Alicia Keys song, like "You're doing a good job," just to show them like that you're really superheroes and you're doing amazing things.

Primary action of leaders during a crisis is connecting with teachers and staff, and, in this case, principals connected with their staff by finding ways to care for them and appreciate them during the COVID-19 crisis.

In a time of crisis, principals should be attentive to their nonverbal behaviors. Nonverbal positive behavior enhances the emotional support of staff, and this emotional support reduces the teachers' stress and anxiety (Jia et al., 2017). The types of nonverbal positive behavior associated with enhanced emotional experience include smiling, nodding, appreciation, and affirming/encouraging gestures. A principal from Florida stated, "I don't sweat the small stuff, and I remain positive and hopeful. I never let my teachers see me upset. I am always smiling and upbeat." Another principal from New York added, "I remain positive and calm. My teachers take their cue from me—if I am calm, smiling, and reassuring, then they will know things will be okay." By exhibiting nonverbal positive and supportive behaviors, principals in a crisis relay a message of hope and optimism that things are going to be okay.

Connecting with Students

Another finding from the COVID-19 leadership study was that principals were determined to maintain a school connection with students. A principal from Minnesota asserted, "I think the two things that are really, really key are those collaborative team planning meetings with everybody involved, and the 10-minute connection with every child every day . . . But the biggest piece is the individual connection to students every day." In a time of crisis, principals realize how important maintaining a positive relationship with students is to the school community. A principal from Connecticut commented,

> With the building closed, it would be easy to just move on and worry about students in the fall, but the kids still needed us, so I ensured that every teacher made contact with students either by phone or video three times a week.

All of the principals agreed that maintaining connections with students was imperative and stressed that students still needed a supportive and caring teacher.

As crisis leaders, principals reacted to the COVID-19 pandemic by creating systems of support for students, but one of the key learnings from the leadership study is that principals must be proactive in building the capacity of their staff to respond to crises. By establishing a culture of care on campus and ensuring every child has a positive relationship with their teachers, principals ensure that their staff will respond in like during a crisis, and students will remain connected to the school.

Leading Across: Connecting with Stakeholders Outside of the School

Enactment of sound leadership and management practices, such as connecting with outside stakeholders, can be drawn upon in a crisis. A Minnesota principal captured the intensity of working with stakeholders during a crisis:

> So I was getting the feedback from all of them and the connection with each one of them in a lot of different ways, in a collective and individually. I don't think there was one most important. I think always the students and the staff and the families, every one of them is truly important. So making sure that I was supporting them . . . And I think the meetings that we had collectively and individually, I was supporting them. They knew they could connect with me at any time. There was a lot of stuff going on and then it was the academics just went away. The academics just went away.

During a crisis, principals need to balance the emergencies that arise and address the immediate concerns of stakeholders. Maintaining connections with outside stakeholders is imperative for principals to acquire the necessary resources needed to support students and families.

A principal during a crisis also needs a peer network to draw upon that is based on trust and honest communication about problems of practice and challenges their school is facing (Leithwood, 2019). A principal in the COVID-19 study described their network support, "A tool that I have for keeping my balance is to be in touch with other administrators each day through a group text or email. We check in with each other often and can share concerns." Another principal from Ohio stated, "I stayed connected with other principals and did weekly check-ins with other principals via calling or texting—just to unwind or get advice." A principal from Tennessee mentioned that her rural school network was a support for her and stated, "The other principals in similar communities, who understood the problems I was facing and offered advice, were supportive and helpful. It made me feel like I wasn't in this alone."

Principal peer-networks are particularly important in a crisis, as they can be nimble and provide feedback and discussion to handle what is relevant and needed at that time (Baker, 2014). Moreover, Baker (2014) purports that technology has enhanced peer communication by shortening the communication distance between peers. Although our observation is that educators have become weary of continuous Zoom interactions, it does allow connections and networking between a larger group of peers such as those in other states, countries, and professional organizations. The rapid information flow between peers is vital to the principal in a crisis and might lead to the survival of the connected (Baker, 2014).

Building a network of peers should be developed and nurtured before a crisis and then continue after the emergency is over. When asked about supportive collegial peer relationships during the COVID-19 crisis, one principal enthusiastically commented, "My colleagues are great, and we shared, you know, had meetings every week and we were always talking. So yep, that was very helpful." While principals are in a network with their peers, some develop their leadership skills and become more influential than others.

According to Leithwood (2019), principals who emerge as a leader among leaders arise from several factors: the principal has a) the ability to exercise influence up the bureaucracy on behalf of the group; b) the expertise to network with colleagues; c) a high degree of emotional intelligence, and d) experience. Experienced principals should be especially attentive to inexperienced administrators. Novice principals or principals with limited experience typically are overwhelmed by the number of issues and stakeholder connections that arise and are amplified during a crisis (Prado Tuma and Spillane, 2019).

CONCLUSION

In 1999, one of the worst U.S. school crises occurred in Columbine, Colorado when two students engaged in a mass shooting at the local high school. Although the principal, Frank Angelis, wanted to resign and heal from this horrific tragedy, he felt an enormous burden to rebuild his school community and restore trust and pride in the high school (Andone, 2019). Over the years, Frank Angelis exemplified the attributes of a meta-leader by addressing the needs of the community and connecting all stakeholders in a common purpose to restore faith in the school. Like Frank Angelis, many principals emerge as meta-leaders during a time of crisis, and they lead because they feel called upon to serve and care for others.

During a crisis, principals are called upon to address the critical issues that arise and take immediate action; however, principals must also balance these emergencies against the long-range purpose and goals of the school. Regardless of the crisis at hand, eventually, it will be resolved, and schools will once again return to their ultimate purpose: teaching and learning.

Perhaps the most important lesson in how principals respond in a time of crisis is how they lead in times of normalcy. If principals are servant leaders who practice their emotional intelligence skills in their daily interactions with stakeholders, then chances are, they will respond with high emotional intelligence during a crisis. Likewise, if principals are effective at creating and maintaining connections with all stakeholders every day, then these connections will naturally occur during a crisis. Every single day matters, and principals who are meta-leaders know and understand that fact. A principal from Texas mentioned that he just went on "autopilot" when the school building closed, and he responded the way he would on any given day: "I took care of my teachers, and I took care of my students." Principals never know when a crisis will hit, but those who are meta-leaders will be prepared to respond effectively and take care of their schools and stakeholders.

POST-NOTE

- In this chapter, we assert that the daily leadership practices of principals are a precursor to how principals will respond during a crisis. Do you agree? Why or why not?
- The current crisis will eventually pass, but what ongoing actions and professional development should leaders undertake to be prepared for the next event?
- Provide a leadership example from your experience during a school crisis. What specific organizational skills were most effectively evidenced by the principal?
- Our chapter presented information that is similar and different from other authors in the book. Analyze what common themes run through the chapter and what themes are unique to an author's viewpoint and why.

REFERENCES

Andone, D. (2019, April 20). 20 years after columbine, former principal Frank De-Angelis is still learning how to move on. *CNN*. https://www.cnn.com/2019/04/20/us/columbine-shooting-anniversary-principal-frank-deangelis-20-years/index.html.

Baker, M. N. (2014). *Peer-to-peer leadership: Why the network is the leader*. ProQuest Ebook Central. https://ebookcentral-proquest-com.proxy.lib.utk.edu.

Burkett, J., and Hayes, S. D. (2018). Campus administrators' responses to Donald Trump's immigration policy: Leadership during times of uncertainty. *International Journal of Educational Leadership and Management*, 6(2), 98–125. http://dx.doi.org/10.17583/ijelm.2018.3602.

Collie, R. J. (2020). The development of social and emotional competence at school: An integrated model. *International Journal of Behavioral Development*, 44(1), 76–87. https://doi.org/10.1177/0165025419851864.

Crews, C. (2020). Foresight and the COVID-19 pandemic. *Research-Technology Management*, 63(4), 55–57. https://doi.org/10.1080/08956308.2020.1762448.

Foste, E. A., and Botero, I. C. (2012). Personal reputation: Effects of upward communication on impressions about new employees. *Management Communication Quarterly*, 26(1), 48–73. https://doi.org/10.1177/0893318911411039.

Fullan, M. (2014). *The principal: Three keys to maximize impact*. Jossey Bass.

Gigliotti, R. A. (2016). Leader as performer; leader as human: A discursive and retrospective construction of crisis leadership. *Atlantic Journal of Communication*, 24(4), 185–200. https://doi.org/10.1080/15456870.2016.1208660.

Glanz, J. (2006). *What every principal should know about cultural leadership*. Corwin.

Goleman, D. (2011). *The brain and emotional intelligence: New Insights*. More than Sound LLC.

Goleman, D., Boyatzis, R., and McKee, A. (2002). *Primal leadership*. Harvard Business School Press.

Greenleaf, R. L. (2002). *Servant leadership: A journey into the nature of legitimate power and greatness*. Paulist Press.

Hatch, T., (2015). Connections, coherence, and common understanding in the common core. In J.A. Supovitz and J. Spillane (Eds.), *Challenging standards: Navigating conflict and building capacity in the era of the Common Core* (pp. 103–11). Rowman and Littlefield.

Jia, M., Cheng, J., and Hale, C. L. (2017). Workplace emotion and communication: Supervisor non-verbal immediacy, employees' emotion experience, and their communication motives. *Management Communication Quarterly*, 31(1), 69–87. https://doi.org/10.1177/0893318916650519.

Kapucu, N., and Ustun, Y. (2018). Collaborative crisis management and leadership in the public sector. *International Journal of Public Administration*, 41(7), 548–61. https://doi.org/10.1080/01900692.2017.1280819

Kouzes, J., and Posner, B. (2007). *The leadership challenge* (fourth edition). Jossey-Bass Publishers.

Leithwood, K. (2019). Characteristics of effective leadership networks: A replication and extension, *School Leadership and Management*, *39*(2), 175–97. https://doi.org/10.1080/13632434.2018.1470503.

Marcus, L. J., McNulty, E. J., Henderson, J. M., and Dorn, B. C. (2019). *Crisis, change, and how to lead when it matters most: You're it.* Hachette Book Group.

Maxwell, L.D., and Superville, D.R (2020, September 12). COVID-19 may drive principals to quit. *Education Week.* https://blogs.edweek.org/edweek/District_Dossier/2020/08/pandemic_principals_quit.html.

Mumford, M. D., Zaccaro, S. J., Harding, F. D., Jacobs, T. O., and Fleishamn, E. A. (2000). Leadership skills for a changing world: Solving complex social problems. *Leadership Quarterly*, *11*(1), 11–35. https://doi.org/10.1016/S1048-9843(99)00041-7.

Prado Tuma, A., and Spillane, J. P. (2019). Novice school principals constructing their role vis-a-vis external stakeholders: (Not) attempting to be "All Things to All People." *Educational Administration Quarterly*, *55*(5), 812–40. https://doi.org/10.1177/0013161X18822101.

Rodriguez, M. A., Murakami-Ramalho, E., and Ruff, W. G. (2009). Leading with heart: Urban elementary principals as advocates for students. *Educational Considerations*, *36*(2), 8–13.

Schneider, J. (2017). *Beyond test scores.* Harvard University Press.

Smylie, M. (2016). Commentary: Three organizational lessons for school district improvement. In K. S. Finnigan and A. J. Daly (Eds.), *Thinking and acting systemically: Improving school districts under pressure* (pp. 209–20). American Educational Research Association.

Spears, L. C. (2010). Character and servant leadership: Ten characteristics of effective, caring leaders. *The Journal of Virtues and Leadership*, *1*(1), 25–30.

Waldron, V. R. (1999). Communication practices of followers, members, and proteges: The cause of upward influence tactics. In M. E. Roloff (Ed.), *Communication Yearbook Volume 22* (pp. 251–99). Sage.

Zaccaro, S. J. (2007). Trait-based perspectives of leadership. *American Psychologist*, *62(1)*, 6–16. https://doi.org/10.1037/0003-066X.62.1.6.

Zepeda, S., Derrington, M. L., and Lanoue, P. (2020). *Developing the organizational culture of the central office: Collaboration, connectivity, and coherence.* Routledge.

Chapter Eight

Changing Educational Paradigms through Distance Learning

Challenges and Opportunities During and After School Crises

Shmuel Shenhav and Ayal Geffon

PRE-FOCUS GUIDING QUESTIONS

- What are the advantages and disadvantages of distance learning in comparison to face-to-face classroom teaching?
- What changes need to be implemented in K–12 education to enhance schools' adaptation to the realities of the twenty-first century?
- How can school crises encourage pedagogical change?
- How should school leaders promote pedagogical change during and after a school crisis?

INTRODUCTION

The need to adapt teaching methods to suit twenty-first-century expectations has been at the forefront of educational research and debate for two decades. Effecting major changes in school practice requires adopting new and often changing educational paradigms (Blass, 2018; Orakcı, 2020). However, changing educational paradigms and practices is an uphill battle (Kovacs, 2017), as school leaders must fight against both bureaucratic constraints and teachers' inclination to teach as they were taught.

The COVID-19 pandemic led to worldwide closures of schools and universities, quickly evolving into a testing ground for online and distance learning, as school leaders and faculty were forced to rethink the aims and methods of schooling to adapt to the crisis. While an exhaustive examination of the results and implications of crisis pedagogy requires a long-term perspective, it is already possible to derive some conclusions from this experience.

Preliminary data indicate that the transition to online learning cannot be simplified as a "success" or a "failure" (Henriksen et al., 2020). Rather, this transition provides insight into the ability of educational leaders and faculty to adjust their educational aims to fit the situation and its impact on teaching. When educators successfully adapt their paradigms to the necessities of crisis pedagogy, the challenges of distance learning become an opportunity to further the learning process.

This chapter explores the ramifications of crisis pedagogy for the future of education and the critical role school leaders play in this effort. The chapter commences with a brief overview of the concepts, aims, and paradigms of twenty-first-century learning as they relate to the concepts of online and distance teaching. Then an analysis of some preliminary data concerning the experience of school leaders and teachers with distance learning during the first phase of the COVID-19 pandemic is made. Lastly, the chapter discusses insights learned from this pandemic that can inform the future of teaching and pedagogic leadership, as school leaders strive to turn challenges into opportunities.

EDUCATIONAL PARADIGMS IN THE TWENTY-FIRST CENTURY

The twentieth century saw the gradual transition of Western society from an agricultural and labor-oriented society, in which high craftsmanship was the trademark of success, to an industrial society that required the knowledge and skills to oversee and manage large enterprises. While the following dictum suffers from overgeneralization, it can be said that twentieth-century learning was characterized as the standardized transmission of the knowledge and skills required to become an effective member of the workforce. The frontal, lecture-mode classroom teaching that was a hallmark of the times may well have seemed suited to this objective.

With the onset of the twenty-first century and the increase in digitalization and automation, standardized knowledge and skills have gradually become irrelevant, as knowledge is digitally available and human skills are replaced by artificial intelligence. Twentieth-century skills have been replaced by the ability to correctly identify problems and the means of resolving them; to access, identify, and critically analyze the relevant information; to efficiently utilize digital resources; and to work individually and collaboratively until a successful resolution of the problem is achieved.

Schleicher (2012) defined four skills as the core of twenty-first-century learning: critical thinking, communication, collaboration, and creativity. Others identify six dimensions, collectively referred to as "deeper learning skills" (Martinez and McGrath, 2014), which include the ability to learn how to learn (Hewlett Foundation, 2013; Huberman et al., 2014). Many other definitions have been suggested (see, e.g., OECD, 2005; Trilling and Fadel, 2009), but the common theme of the different definitions is the importance of encouraging autonomous learning and self-motivation.

The concepts of student-autonomy and self-motivation are interrelated and an essential component of effective learning. The copious work of Ryan and Deci (e.g., 2000, 2017, 2020) on self-determination theory and its applications shows that successful learners need to feel that they are instigating their learning and to feel a sense of freedom in their activities. The greater the sense of autonomy, the more the pupils are motivated to apply effort to their studies.

Closely related to the autonomy-supportive classroom is the concept of differentiated instruction (Tomlinson, 2017; Tomlinson and Murphy, 2015). According to the paradigm of differentiated instruction, effective teaching requires adapting the content and the means of learning to each student's abilities, interests, and modes of learning. Rather than focusing on curriculum-based content, teaching focuses on the student, on their needs and abilities (Butcher and Wilson-Strydon, 2008; Jones, 2007).

Fostering an autonomy-supportive and student-oriented classroom atmosphere requires a shift in the teachers' perception of their role: Instead of serving as the expert and tutor, the teacher serves as a mentor and educational support for the learner (Butcher and Wilson-Strydon, 2008; Hoidn, 2017).

In the physical classroom, this is easier said than done. Even when teachers have undergone professional development in the field and conceptually embrace the concept of an autonomy-supportive classroom, such endeavors are liable to fail or peter out due to administrative constraints, inflexible curricula, high-stakes testing, and teachers' perceptions of the complexities involved in controlling the autonomy-supportive classroom. Often, human nature simply reverts to tried and proven practices.

Conversely, online and distance learning provide both the impetus and the means to successfully implement autonomous learning and differentiated instruction (Christensen et al., 2016; Hadjerrouit, 2010). While the physical classroom naturally draws students and teachers into a single group focused on a single activity or lecture, distance learning defaults to individual learning. Classes and groups must be artificially created, and it is as simple to create diverse groups and learning modes as it is to create a single classroom. Zipori (2020) suggests focusing on the learners' current topics of interest, which necessarily encourages diversifying the learning experience according to the inclinations of the learners.

This is especially true with asynchronous teaching, where each student learns at their own time and pace and with individual activities. However, it will be shown below that crisis pedagogy offers the opportunity to implement differentiated instruction even through synchronous learning in the virtual classroom.

Although distance learning is naturally suited to student-oriented pedagogy, its implementation cannot be taken for granted. Koehler et al. (2014) discusses the "technological pedagogical content knowledge framework" (TPACK), in which successful online learning is dependent on the teacher's mastery of these three facets: technological literacy, the pedagogy of distance learning, and the content of the lesson.

The SAMR model (Puentedura, 2006) proposes four levels of implementing technology in teaching: *substitution* (where technology substitutes standard teaching with no functional change), *augmentation* (where technology enhances functionality), modification (where technology enables redesigning lessons), and *redefinition* (where technology creates new methods of teaching). Of these, only the last two levels of implementation might involve pedagogical change, and a critical analysis of the SAMR model illustrates that even *redefinition* does not necessarily incorporate a fundamentally different approach to teaching (Hamilton et al., 2016).

Educating in the twenty-first century calls for a new pedagogy that encourages autonomous learners and shifts the focus from the teacher to the student. Such pedagogies are not always easily implemented. Distance learning provides the means for student-oriented teaching. However, without paradigmatic change, distance learning remains a poor substitute for face-to-face classroom teaching. Times of crises exacerbate the need for paradigmatic change, but also provide a unique opportunity to truly put new pedagogies into practice.

DISTANCE LEARNING DURING THE FIRST PHASE OF THE COVID-19 PANDEMIC

While distance learning remains the lesser-used option during times of stability, at times of crises (e.g., war, pandemics, or natural calamities) it may be the only option available. Crisis pedagogy requires not only adapting to practical limitations such as the inability to reach the physical classroom but also to the emotional and cognitive limitations of learners under emotional stress in a VUCA (Volatile, Uncertain, Complex, Ambiguous) world (Hadar et al., 2020).

The COVID-19 pandemic serves as an extreme example of crisis pedagogy. In March–April 2020, the pandemic's swift onset caused the rapid closure of schools throughout the world and the transition to emergency distance learning. This transition was largely characterized by a lack of readiness and an attempt to ensure educational continuity despite the constant uncertainty (Cohen and Davidovitch, 2020; Hodges et al., 2020). Many teachers had no former experience with distance teaching, and even those who expressed familiarity with technological tools were generally lacking in pedagogical awareness (Gudmundsdottir and Hathaway, 2020).

Among the challenges encountered during the initial transition period were the difficulty of learning via computer for lengthy periods, parents' struggle to combine work with facilitating homeschooling, digital inequity due both to technologically challenged learners and disparity in the availability of technological resources, and the psychological impact of "social distancing" practices enacted in an attempt to halt the spread of the pandemic (Cohen and Davidovitch, 2020; Donitsa-Schmidt and Ramot, 2020; Hall et al., 2020; Jæger and Blaabæk, 2020).

In these circumstances, a student-oriented pedagogy is essential: a pedagogy that cares for the individuals' success in their unique circumstances, and concerns itself not only with the learners' academic achievements but with their emotional well-being. Preliminary data concerning the experience of school leaders and teachers during the first phase of the pandemic provides some insights into the implementation of a student-oriented pedagogy. As part of an ongoing study on the way in which teachers and students coped with the challenges of the transition to distance learning, the authors conducted semi-structured interviews with twenty-five teachers in Israel. The following teachers' perceptions emerged from an analysis of the data:

- In times of crises, and perhaps in times of stability too, ensuring the individual's progress should take priority over meeting curricula demands. With the focus on autonomous learning, brief lessons with small groups that enable the teacher to reach out to each student and support their studies are often preferable to full-length lessons to an entire class.
- Distance learning can easily enable student-oriented pedagogy through asynchronous teaching. Different assignments can be set depending on the student's ability, inclination, and available resources. However, if the teacher is focused on the students, the synchronous, virtual classroom also provides a student-oriented experience. As one student expressed it:

    When I see the teacher on the screen, looking directly at me, I feel as though they are speaking to *me*, teaching *me*, almost like a private lesson.

> The intimacy is far greater than in the physical classroom, even though I know that many other students are present too.

- Teachers expressed the importance of showing faith in the learners' ability to cope with autonomous learning. Believing in one's students is important in any pedagogical context (Boone et al., 2006), and even more so when students are expected to govern their own learning. During the transition to autonomous learning, it is essential.
- While digital literacy is important, a strong student-oriented pedagogy can often overcome technological limitations. Teachers who taught in technologically challenged sectors described successful experiences employing low-technology methods, for example, telephone recordings, email, and even fax machines, provided that these were supplemented by personal contact with each student to ensure their comprehension of the material.
- Student-oriented pedagogy does not mean merely ensuring that students have resources and guidance suited to their circumstances and abilities. It means concerning oneself with each student's success and well-being. In one documented instance, a teacher repeated the entire lesson for a single student who had been uninformed of the scheduled lesson in the virtual classroom.

IMPLICATIONS FOR THE FUTURE OF TEACHING AND PEDAGOGIC LEADERSHIP

Ensuring effective pedagogy is a central aspect of school leaders' responsibility, as discussed by Haim Shaked in chapter 6 of this volume. While teachers are directly responsible for implementing pedagogical change, their ability and inclination to do so is largely dependent on school leaders' priorities and directives.

During times of crises, school leaders must ensure that the concept of "no child left behind" continues to apply in the broadest sense, encouraging teachers to implement student-oriented pedagogy, to explore creative methods of engaging students in distance learning, and to concern themselves with their students' success, progress, and well-being.

However, pedagogical change should not be limited to a time of crisis. Distance learning is unlikely to continue to the same extent once the crisis is resolved, but the paradigmatic shift from content-oriented teaching to student-oriented teaching should not dissipate with the successful resolution of worldwide or nationwide crises or be merely set aside in readiness for the next crisis. While a completely student-oriented pedagogy may be impractical to implement in the standard classroom, it is imperative that the fundamental concepts and paradigms discovered through crisis pedagogy be preserved and internalized.

Teachers and school leaders must remember that personal crises are a constant occurrence, requiring flexibility and a student-oriented and concerned pedagogy to enable them to succeed. Even without crises, many students do not fit easily into the Procrustean bed of set curricula and standardization. However, student-oriented teaching is important not only for those students. As discussed above, autonomous learning and fostering the ability to learn how to learn are at the core of the skills necessary to succeed in the twenty-first century. Consequently, the paradigmatic shift toward student-oriented and autonomous learning is a revolution waiting to happen.

The onus this places upon school leaders is not a light one. Often during a time of crisis, little guidance can be provided to school leaders as to the required pedagogical steps (Harris and Jones, 2020). Former organizational norms regarding decision-making processes and leadership hierarchies may become irrelevant. The external pressures shaping society as a whole at a time of crisis impact on the school culture, shaping it anew (Smith and Riley, 2012).

In a VUCA world, characterized as volatile, uncertain, complex, and ambiguous, Johansen (2007) proposes four parallel facets of leadership, known as the VUCA-Prime model: *vision, understanding, clarity,* and *agility.* Of these four facets, agility is the most relevant to school crisis leadership. School leaders need to embrace an adaptive leadership approach, collaborating with other stakeholders to learn and guide concomitantly (Drago-Severson and Blum-DeStefano, 2018).

Furthermore, the very nature of student-oriented pedagogy precludes the possibility of directing teachers down a specific path. Each teacher must decide on the most appropriate methodologies depending on the needs of their students. School leaders are therefore required to guide without coercion and to encourage paradigmatic awareness without stipulating a specific manner of implementation. Reimers and Schleicher (2020) recommend establishing a steering committee to develop an educational response to crises. Such a committee can provide a wider perspective as to the needs and abilities of the students and present suggestions that may aid teachers in formulating their own response.

CONCLUSION

Crisis pedagogy and crisis leadership require unique skills, which are often lacking. Rather than hope that the mantle is taken up by naturally talented individuals, teacher-education and leadership programs should provide professional development in these areas, enabling current and future teachers and school leaders to discuss relevant ideas, practices, and ways of thought. As we live in a VUCA world, such programs should be implemented in advance and not just with the onset of crises. Simulation-based teaching (Erlam et al., 2017; Poikela and Poikela, 2012; Tiwari et al., 2014) might be used to encourage education and leadership students to experiment with crisis pedagogy and crisis leadership in a safe, virtual environment, encouraging individualized and situational responses to a crisis.

Crisis leadership requires school leaders to adopt an open leadership style, to be attentive to teachers' suggestions, to encourage them to implement such pedagogical changes as they deem appropriate, to stress that they are at the staffs' disposal, and to aid them to the best of their ability. Ultimately, crisis leadership leads not from the front, but from behind.

POST-NOTE

- In this chapter, it is contended that student-oriented pedagogy is generally more effective and better suited to the realities of the twenty-first century than content-oriented pedagogy. Do you agree? What arguments can be presented to favor a content-oriented pedagogy?
- We suggest that despite, and because of, the immense challenges involved in distance learning during crises, crisis pedagogy can become an opportunity to improve pedagogical thinking and ultimately, to improve educational experiences. What are your experiences with crisis pedagogy? What advantages can you perceive in crisis pedagogy through your own experiences?
- This chapter indicates ways in which distance and online learning have greater potential than traditional, classroom learning. To what extent do you think that distance learning can truly supplant classroom learning? Why? What are the hurdles that must be overcome to fully implement the concepts outlined in this chapter?
- As a school leader, how does your experience leading schools through crisis pedagogy compare with the ideas presented in this chapter?

REFERENCES

Blass, E. (2018). White paper: A 21st century education paradigm. *Journal of Education and Social Policy*, 5(3), 128–33. http://doi.org/10.30845/jesp.v5n3p16.

Boone, E., Hartzman, M., and Mero, D. (2006). Believing in student achievement. *Principal Leadership*, 6(10), 21–25.

Butcher, N., and Wilson-Strydon, M. (2008). Technology and open learning: The potential of open education resources for k-12 education. In J. Voogt and G. Knezek (Eds.), *International handbook of information technology in primary and secondary education* (pp. 725–45). Springer Science and Business Media.

Christensen, C., Horn, M., and Johnson, C. (2016). *Disrupting class: How innovation will change the way the world learns.* McGraw-Hill.

Cohen, E., and Davidovitch, N. (2020). The development of online learning in Israeli higher education. *Journal of Education and Learning, 9*(5), 15–26. https://doi.org/10.5539/jel.v9n5p15.

Donitsa-Schmidt, S., and Ramot, R. (2020) Opportunities and challenges: Teacher education in Israel in the Covid-19 pandemic, *Journal of Education for Teaching*, https://doi.org/10.1080/02607476.2020.1799708.

Drago-Severson, E., and Maslin-Ostrowski, P. (2018). In translation: School leaders learning in and from leadership practice while confronting pressing policy challenges. *Teachers College Record, 120*(1), 1–44.

Erlam, G. D., Smythe, L., and Wright-St Clair, V. (2017). Simulation is not a pedagogy. *Open Journal of Nursing, 7,* 779–87. https://doi.org/10.4236/ojn.2017.77059.

Gudmundsdottir, G. B., and Hathaway, D. M. (2020). "We always make it work": Teachers' agency in the time of crisis. *Journal of Technology and Teacher Education, 28*(2), 239–50. https://www.learntechlib.org/primary/p/216242/.

Hadar, L. L., Ergas, O., Alpert, B., and Ariav, T. (2020). Rethinking teacher education in a VUCA world: student teachers' social-emotional competencies during the Covid-19 crisis. *European Journal of Teacher Education,* 1–14. https://doi.org/10.1080/02619768.2020.1807513.

Hadjerrouit, S. (2010). A conceptual framework for using and evaluating web-based learning resources in school education. *Journal of Information Technology Education, 9,* 53–79. https://doi.org/10.28945/1106.

Hall, T., Connolly, C., Ó Grádaigh, S., Burden, K., Kearney, M., Schuck, S., Bottema, J., Cazemier, G., Hustinx, W., Evens, M., Koenraad, T., Makridou, E., and Kosmas, P. (2020). Education in precarious times: A comparative study across six countries to identify design priorities for mobile learning in a pandemic. *Information and Learning Sciences.* https://doi.org/10.1108/ILS-04-2020-0089.

Hamilton, E. R., Rosenberg, J. M., and Akcaoglu, M. (2016). The substitution augmentation modification redefinition (SAMR) model: A critical review and suggestions for its use. *TechTrends, 60*(5), 433–41. https://doi.org/10.1007/s11528-016-0091-y.

Harris, A., and Jones, M. (2020). COVID 19 – school leadership in disruptive times. *School Leadership and Management, 40*(4), 243–47. https://doi.org/10.1080/13632434.2020.1811479.

Henriksen, D., Creely, E., and Henderson, M. (2020). Folk pedagogies for teacher transitions: approaches to synchronous online learning in the wake of COVID-19. *Journal of Technology and Teacher Education, 28*(2), 201–9. https://www.learntechlib.org/primary/p/216179/.

Hewlett Foundation (2013). *Deeper learning competencies.* http://www.hewlett.org/uploads/documents/Deeper_Learning_Defined__April_2013.pdf.

Hodges, C., Moore, S., Lockee, B., Trust, T., and Bond, A. (2020). The difference between emergency remote teaching and online learning. *Educause Review, 27*. https://er.educause.edu/articles/2020/3/the-difference-between-emergency-remote-teaching-and-online-learning.

Hoidn, S. (2017). *Student-centered learning environments in higher education classrooms*. Palgrave Macmillan.

Huberman, M., Bitter, C., Anthony, J., and O'Day, J. (2014). *The shape of deeper learning: Strategies, structures, and cultures in deeper learning network high schools*. American Institute for Research. https://files.eric.ed.gov/fulltext/ED553360.pdf.

Jæger, M. M., and Blaabæk, E. H. (2020). Inequality in learning opportunities during Covid-19: Evidence from library takeout. *Research in Social Stratification and Mobility, 68*, 100524. https://doi.org/10.1016/j.rssm.2020.100524.

Johansen, R. (2007). *Get there early: Sensing the future to compete in the present*. Berrett-Koehler.

Jones, L. (2007). *The student-centered classroom*. Cambridge University Press.

Koehler, M. J., Mishra, P., Kereluik, K., Shin, T. S., and Graham, C. R. (2014). The technological pedagogical content knowledge framework. In J. Spector, M. Merrill, J. Elen, and M. Bishop (Eds.), *Handbook of research on educational communications and technology*. Springer. https://doi.org/10.1007/978-1-4614-3185-5_9.

Kovacs, H. (2017). Learning and teaching in innovation: Why it is important for education in 21st century. *Neveléstudomány Tanulmányok, 2*, 45–60. http://doi.org/10.21549/NTNY.18.2017.2.4.

Martinez, M. R., and McGrath, D. (2014). *Deeper Learning: How eight innovative public schools are transforming education in the twenty-first century*. The New Press.

OECD (2005). *The definition and selection of key competencies*. OECD. https://www.oecd.org/pisa/35070367.pdf.

Orakcı, S. (Ed.). (2020). *Paradigm shifts in 21st century teaching and learning*. IGI Global. http://doi:10.4018/978-1-7998-3146-4.

Poikela, E., and Poikela, P. (Eds.). (2012). *Towards simulation pedagogy: Developing nursing simulation in a European network*. Rovaniemi University of Applied Sciences Publications.

Puentedura, R. (2006). *Transformation, technology, and education*. http://hippasus.com/resources/tte/.

Reimers, F. M., and Schleicher, A. (2020). A framework to guide an education response to the COVID-19 pandemic of 2020. OECD. https://www.hm.ee/sites/default/files/framework_guide_v1_002_harward.pdf.

Ryan, R. M., and Deci, E. L. (2000). Intrinsic and extrinsic motivations: Classic definitions and new directions. *Contemporary Educational Psychology, 25*, 54–67. https://doi.org/10.1006/ceps.1999.1020.

Ryan, R. M., and Deci, E. L. (2017). *Self-determination theory: Basic psychological needs in motivation, development, and wellness*. Guilford Publishing.

Ryan, R. M., and Deci, E. L. (2020). Intrinsic and extrinsic motivation from a self-determination theory perspective: Definitions, theory, practices, and future directions. *Contemporary Educational Psychology, 61.* https://doi.org/10.1016/j.cedpsych.2020.101860.

Schleicher, A. (Ed.). (2012). *Preparing teachers and developing school leaders for the 21st century: Lessons from around the world.* OECD Publishing. https://www.oecd.org/site/eduistp2012/49850576.pdf.

Smith, L., and Riley, D. (2012). School leadership in times of crisis. *School Leadership and Management, 32*(1), 57–71. https://doi.org/10.1080/13632434.2011.614941.

Tiwari, S. R., Nafees, L., and Krishnan, O. (2014). Simulation as a pedagogical tool: Measurement of impact on perceived effective learning. *The International Journal of Management Education, 12*(3), 260–70. https://doi.org/10.1016/j.ijme.2014.06.006.

Tomlinson, C. A. (2017). *How to differentiate instruction in academically diverse classrooms* (third edition). ASCD.

Tomlinson, C. A., and Murphy, M. (2015). *Leading for differentiation: Growing teachers who grow kids.* ASCD.

Trilling, B., and Fadel, C. (2009). *21st century skills: Learning for life in our times.* Jossey-Bass.

Zipori, O. (2020). Toward a presentist pedagogy of interest. *Educational Theory.* https://doi.org/10.1111/edth.12396.

Chapter Nine

The Impact of School Crises on Students and Families from a Social-Justice Perspective

Practical Suggestions for Teachers and Principals

Katia Gonzáles

PRE-FOCUS GUIDING QUESTIONS

- Based on some major crisis that affected your school, discuss its impact on students, families, and educators.
- How can you as a principal mitigate or resolve any negative impact of the crisis you discussed in the item above?
- How can families, schools, and communities collaborate to establish effective partnerships to support students' growth during a crisis?
- Based on your knowledge of the issue of social justice, how can it inform a principal's perspective in dealing with a crisis?

INTRODUCTION

Historically, schools everywhere have been exposed to a myriad of crises in which swift action by teachers and other school leaders was needed. The most recent global crisis prompted immediate action at all levels of leadership. The impact of having to close all schools due to the COVID-19 pandemic in the United States, and probably all over the world, engaged stakeholders in a national conversation on ways to address, in a more systematic manner, equitable educational experiences for students. "The COVID-19 pandemic is overwhelming the functioning and outcomes of education systems—some of which were already stressed in many respects" (Garcia and Weiss, 2020, p.3). A public health crisis of this magnitude highlighted the many ways in which societal inequities, together with specific economic and health concerns, directly impacted students, families, teachers, and communities (Garcia and Weiss, 2020).

Individuals working in school systems, specifically teachers, staff, and administrators, were confronted with a most challenging endeavor of addressing students' individual needs in a system that had been plagued with inequities for years. The COVID-19 pandemic brought to light ways in which students, but particularly students from underrepresented groups, have been the most vulnerable. Students' access to specific technological resources and instructional supports, available and reliable caregivers, food shortages, and the uncertainty of the future were troubling and, in many cases, exacerbated given the magnitude of the crisis. Experts warned of the long-lasting socioemotional as well as educational effects this pandemic could have on students' overall mental health and education. Kuhfeld, Soland, Tarasawa, Johnson, Rusek, and Liu (2020) indicated how "while the scale of the COVID-19 school closures is novel, the inequalities in our school systems are unfortunately anything but new. Our models cannot account for the reality that the crisis is having an unequal impact on our most underserved communities" (p. 28).

But children weren't the only ones stressed. Russell, Hutchison, Tambling, Tomkunas, and Horton (2020) explained that it is not uncommon for parents caring for children, especially during a traumatic event such as a pandemic, to experience a variety of stressors possibly impacting their own self-care and parent-child dynamics. Parents reported that their stress levels skyrocketed having to navigate between meeting the emotional and academic needs of their children, while trying to run a household and, in many cases, keep working at their job (Catalyst, 2020). Teachers and administrators were certainly confused, frightened, and overwhelmed (Schleicher, 2020).

The COVID-19 pandemic highlighted the need for a national conversation related to ways in which schools could serve as essential hubs for community support and even growth during a crisis. Principals and teachers felt an incredible amount of pressure to advocate for students and families, while also attempting to address their own well-being and personal needs. It was realized that national action was necessary to break down barriers impacting students' success (Noguera, 2020). Clearly, it was evident that when schools are not functioning well, families and communities suffer (Noguera, 2020).

This chapter will focus particularly on the impact a severe crisis can have on students and families. By using a social justice framework, we can understand the urgency and the necessity for providing support to students and their families traumatized, to varying degrees, by a crisis. Teachers and principals play a pivotal role in assisting students and families during a crisis. Strategies and suggestions are offered.

THE CHALLENGE AND THE OPPORTUNITY

During the initial stages of the pandemic and the early school closures, school leaders were asked to make decisions about how to effectively implement and sustain a variety of mitigation measures in anticipation of the safe reopening of schools. Families, particularly those from minority groups, did not always trust the ability of school leaders to make informed and "organized decisions" to support the safe reopening of schools (Eama, 2020), especially in buildings with years of delayed maintenance and schools without adequate funding and resources.

School leaders, often challenged by different messages and inconsistent information sent by boards of education, school boards, or ministries of health, needed to remain calm amid the storm and transmit information to groups of stakeholders in clear and supportive ways. School leaders searched for ways to establish consistent patterns of communication and support to open the lines of communication among all stakeholders and develop feelings of trust. "When school leaders need to make tough calls, a system of governance that values the thoughts of every stakeholders may lead to better outcomes" (Martell, 2020). Gonzáles and Frumkin (2019) discussed that when schools focus on establishing effective communication patterns with stakeholders, opportunities for shared responsibility toward a common goal is often achieved. The authors pinpoint the need for schools to always incorporate culturally responsive practices, together with intercultural connections, in order for effective partnerships and communication to be created.

Farber (2020) explained how the pandemic brought challenging times but also provided stakeholders with opportunities to "pause, reflect, grieve, and decide how we want to move forward" (p. 1). The pandemic also created a noticeable positive change in school practices related to leadership with more open communications with families outside of the school setting. At the same time, society's view regarding the teaching profession, the expertise needed to help students succeed, and ways in which teachers could impact students' lives beyond the classroom also changed. "Public recognition of the essential caretaking role schools play in society has skyrocketed. As young people struggle to learn from home, parents' gratitude for teachers, their skills, and their invaluable role in student well-being has risen" (Vegas and Whintrop, 2020, p. 1). Longmuir (2020) discussed how "there is great potential for positive post-COVID adaptations that could benefit teachers and communities alike. Not the least is building great appreciation, respect for the work of teachers that builds on the enhanced visibility of teachers' work and the stronger connections to families and communities" (p. 17).

Possibilities are endless when members of a group begin to communicate more effectively and openly, and multiple experiences and perspectives are seen as valuable contributions toward a common goal (Gonzáles and Frumkin, 2019). As school leaders took action to develop patterns of communication and opportunities for all voices to be heard, teachers led the way in empowering, communicating, and closely collaborating with families and colleagues to help shape the future of education one day at a time. Teachers took on leadership roles outside of their classroom space and instructional responsibilities by taking swift action to address specific needs while considering ways in which group dynamics and relationship-building could impact practice. Teachers displayed the characteristics typically found in effective school leaders that are leading through a crisis. According to the Australian Institute for Teaching and School Leadership Initiative (2020), effective leaders that lead during a crisis "draw on a toolkit of skills and approaches, which are reactive and proactive; prioritize open communication; proactively triage and manage threats to their community; leverage expertise and experience from multiple stakeholders to facilitate transition from a crisis; work collaboratively to transform and build back better; support the wellbeing of their school community (while maintaining their own well-being)" (p. 1).

Principals also play a key role. The pandemic created a shift in thinking, in which the "traditional" model and view of schooling and school leadership became obsolete. Harris and Jones (2020) described how it was challenging for school leaders to know the impact certain decisions might have stating that "school leaders are walking a tightrope without a safety net. There are no precedents and no guides to leading school in a pandemic" (p. 243). However, school leaders did understand the need to empower and encourage others to lead and take action as they considered the role of "distributive leadership" and ways it could impact practice" (Harris and Jones, 2020, p. 245). Spillane (2005) explained how "rather than viewing leadership practice as a product of a leader's knowledge and skill, the distributed perspective defines it as the interactions between people and their situation" (p. 144).

APPLYING A SOCIAL JUSTICE PERSPECTIVE

The concept of social justice has received wide attention in the literature (see, e.g., Bogotch, 2000; Rapp, 2002; Brown and Shaked, 2018). The subject of promoting social justice in schools is vast, so attention to it in this section will remain introductory. Calls for social justice abound, because many critics over the years have pointed to significant social, political, economic, and educational inequities in schools (see, e.g., Apple, 1988; Spring, 2019).

Schooling, for these critics, perpetuates and reinforces social, racial, and gender stratifications. Inequities in allocations of school finances (Kozol, 2012), socially stratified arrangements through which subject matter is delivered (known as tracking practices) in schools (Oakes, 2005), biased content of the curriculum (Anyon, 1980), patriarchal relations through authority patterns and staffing (Strober and Tyack, 1980), differential distribution of knowledge by gender within classrooms (Sadker and Sadker, 1994), and the influence of teacher expectations (Rosenthal and Jacobson, 1968) are examples of inequities decried by these critics.

Educational exclusionary attitudes and practices have significant pedagogical, curricular, leadership, and moral implications for the work of progressive and idealistic educators as well as concerned community members. These inequities become exacerbated during a crisis. Assessing the impact of a major crisis on students, parents, and educators is greatly informed by a social-justice perspective because assistance, whatever its nature, can be evenly distributed to all groups negatively affected by a crisis. Inclusionary pedagogy, as opposed to historically exclusionary prevalent school practices, becomes the norm, rather than the exception, during a school crisis.

The recent COVID-19 pandemic brought to light ways in which a social-justice perspective can provide a much needed framework to target the negative impact of a crisis on students and families. "Social justice is about distributing resources fairly and treating all students equitably so that they feel safe and secure—physically and psychologically" (Alvarez, 2019). Teachers and school leaders who advocate for social justice are more inclined to remain sensitive to the needs of all students and families impacted by a major school-related crisis (Mundoff et al., 2019). They are also more likely to point out specific barriers impacting students and families and the need to have support at the local and federal level to address pervasive educational inequities.

Brankenridge (2020) mentioned that teachers, operating from a social-justice approach, are experts in relationship building and understand the importance of getting to know students at an individual level and ways to help them connect with peers. During the pandemic, teachers took it upon themselves to nurture the relationships they were building with students and also with families. Teachers know that, especially during the pandemic, "The Three Rs: Relationships, Routines, and Resilience" can make a tremendous difference in an individual's life.

Instructionally, Gershon (2012) explained that these teachers cannot "[facilitate] learning with students and [advocate] for children, without a social justice perspective that brings awareness of the academic needs of underrepresented students. In this light, culturally relevant teaching practices need emphasis. This is because social justice is not a series of steps or practices, but is instead a way of knowing and being" (p. 144). School leaders who recognize the importance of a social-justice perspective "encourage students to take an active role in their own education and support teachers in creating empowering, democratic, and critical educational environments" (Hackman, 2005, p.103) that promote learning for all.

IMPACT OF A MAJOR CRISIS ON STUDENTS AND FAMILIES

The immediate and long-term impact of a crisis of the magnitude of COVID-19 on students and families' overall social and emotional well-being is marked. According to Spinelli, Lionetti, Pastore, and Fasolo (2020), the prolonged lockdown has created an incredible amount of challenges for parents seeking to support their children while managing work-life responsibilities. The authors explain that parental stress could directly trickle down to parent-child dynamics and overall caretaking responsibilities, thus impacting students' mental health and behavior in serious ways. Understanding of the risk factors for families (parents and their children as well as other possible household members) on students' overall growth can be valuable information for teachers and principals seeking to establish effective school-home practices and partnerships.

Further, the pressure many families feel in having to provide daily educational support to their children, in additional to other responsibilities, can serve as a catalyst for an imbalanced work-life situation. "The sudden addition of 'teacher' to a parent's resume does not come easily. To expect parents, who are untrained in the science of education, to become effective educators overnight ignores the expertise required to be a teacher" (Azuara, 2020). A social-justice lens sheds light on various economic disparities as well related to educating children at home. Parents might not have the financial resources to purchase additional laptops or upgrade their internet capacities. Sharing one or even two computers for large families add stressors, emotionally and academically. Black and Hispanic families of lower socioeconomics are particularly impacted by the lack of access to distance-learning resources, reliable internet connections, and computers for effective participation in schools (Auxier and Anderson, 2020).

In addition to stressors related to parent-child dynamics, Xiang, Zhang, and Kuwahara (2020) discussed that the lack of opportunities for children to engage in physical activity increases sedentary behaviors potentially impacting students' mental and physical health for years to come. The authors encouraged stakeholders to consider ways to engage children in more physical activity to support healthy development. Daily physical activities can go a long way to reduce levels of anxiety, alleviate boredom, and increase social bonding among family members.

With many families losing jobs and schools not open as a source of support, food insecurities are also creating additional stressors for many families trying to maintain their children's health. Cronin (2020) explained that people of color, especially Black and Hispanic people, are impacted the most by food insecurities. "A new study from Northwestern University, based on Census Bureau Data, shows that 40% of Black households and 36% of Hispanic households are struggling to afford food. Meanwhile, about 22% of White households are reporting food insecurities" (Cronin, 2020). Access to Supplemental Nutrition Assistance Program (SNAP) is providing some relief to families needing support, but many are now relying on growing their own food as they come to terms with job losses and a lack of essential supports such as the school's food programs (Cronin, 2020).

Research indicates that a family's socioeconomic background and race may also impact their decisions regarding the benefits of schools reopening during a pandemic, creating additional stressors. Saavedra, Rapaport, Silver, Polikoff, Garland, and Haderlein (2020) reported that many families, in particular families of color, are concerned about children physically attending school, getting sick, and having to deal with the consequences of becoming ill potentially overriding any academic benefits of having schools reopen. However, by not having physical access to schools, families are missing out on directly interacting with others to serve as support systems (i.e., homework help, emotional support, parent groups, and interpreters). Families with students with disabilities are also in a very difficult situation, especially if students were receiving school services. Although marginalized groups are most dramatically impacted, even families of means, to varying degrees, are confronted with similar issues.

PRACTICAL SUGGESTIONS FOR TEACHERS AND PRINCIPALS

One of the challenges during and after a major crisis like COVID-19 is that it can widen the achievement gap impacting students and marginalized communities. It is important for teachers and principals to carefully consider a social-justice lens that can serve as a framework to effectively inform decision-making related to pedagogy and effective collaboration with families, students, and community partners. There are so many variables impacting schools and families, and the following is a list of some recommendations for teachers and principals to grapple with during a major school-related crisis:

- Establish a school-community partnership committee to bring in the voices of different stakeholders to help support advocacy and strategic planning to target areas of need and discuss various relief efforts, short-term and long-term. School leaders should not plan and implement support efforts in isolation of these collaborations.
- Create collaborations with families and effective communication structures so that information is dispensed quickly and accurately. School leaders should serve as mediators between local and state authorities that issue updates during a crisis and their communities.
- Support students and their families, especially those from underrepresented groups, with online platforms and high levels of connectivity. Schools can lend families computers that are currently not used to support more effective educational experiences at home.
- Establish a mentor-protégé program for students and parents to connect with other families in supportive ways. This type of mentorship program can also be established for school staff. Principals need to coordinate these efforts via distance-learning technologies. This program should be continued once school operations return to normal.
- Work with families to create a database highlighting community resources important to the community and ways in which these community resources can serve as a support to families, teachers, and students.
- Provide online workshops by professionals (social workers and psychologists) for parents on ways to address their children's anxieties, tensions, and even just basic questions that children of all ages might have that parents alone might not be able to address correctly.
- Make ongoing professional development (PD) for teachers a priority. Teachers need PD related to the use of digital technologies in order to be able to effectively focus on instruction. In addition, teachers can greatly benefit from additional PD on best ways to support students' socioemotional and academic growth, especially for students at risk.
- Form alliances with national and professional organizations to establish networks of support for schools to have opportunities to come together to share best practices and mutual concerns.
- Connect with local universities and community resources, such as the library, to discuss possibilities for partnerships to support students and families (i.e., homework help, specific disciplinary experiences, books and resources, etc.). School leaders can coordinate efforts with local and school

libraries for home delivery of reading books that help to sustain student interest and support students academically.
- Assist teachers, via a social-justice lens, to establish critically reflective working groups to target current issues in social-justice education and ways in which a proactive, and not a reactive, approach could impact teaching and learning. Many teachers may be unfamiliar with various approaches using such a lens that can support learning.
- Finally, and related to the last point, culturally relevant teaching practices should be encouraged. Culturally responsive teachers (Hammond, 2014) make special efforts to get to know their students really well, even via distance learning. Teachers who utilize such teaching practices are sensitive to the educational needs of culturally diverse students. A complete discussion of this latter point goes beyond the discussion here, but school leaders can offer suggestions to teachers via targeted PD.

CONCLUSION

The pandemic served as a disturbing awakening to the realities families and school systems face when attempting to address the educational experiences of students during a crisis. It served as an important reminder that collective responsibility, effective communication, and a social-justice lens can lead to informed decision-making for change. As teachers and principals continue to work on developing educational experiences that are nurturing, supportive, and inclusive, stakeholders must remain vigilant in their willingness and ability to deal with the impact of a severe crisis on students and parents. School leaders must become social, even political activists to advocate for students and families negatively impacted by a crisis.

POST-NOTE

- In what ways have schools in your community addressed the needs of students and families during crises?
- In what ways do you foresee teachers, families, school leaders, students, and community partners collaborating to transform schools to avert the negative effects of a crisis? What does "transformation of schools" mean to you when considering a social-justice approach?
- React to each of the practical suggestions enumerated above. Are they doable in your situation? Explain why or why not.

- What are some additional suggestions for teachers and principals in dealing with and advocating for students and families during crises?

REFERENCES

Alvarez, B. (2019). Why social justice in school matters: Meet five educators who are determined to help young people realize their value and power. *NEA*. https://www.nea.org/advocating-for-change/new-from-nea/why-social-justice-school-matters.

Anyon, J. (1980). Social class and the hidden curriculum. *Journal of Education, 162*(1), 67–92. https://doi.org/10.1177/002205748016200106.

Apple, M. (1988). *Teachers and text: A political economy of class and gender.* Routledge.

Australian Institute for Teaching and School Leadership Initiative (AITSL). (2020). The role of school leadership during challenging times. *Spotlight.* https://www.aitsl.edu.au/research/spotlight/the-role-of-school-leadership-in-challenging-times.

Auxier, B., and Anderson, M. (2020). As schools close due to the coronavirus, some U.S. students face a "digital homework gap." Pew Research Center. https://www.pewresearch.org/fact-tank/2020/03/16/as-schools-close-due-to-the-coronavirus-some-u-s-students-face-a-digital-homework-gap/.

Azuara, M. (2020, August 20). The impact of Covid-19 on working parents [Blog post]. https://bridgepointconsulting.com/the-impact-of-covid-19-on-working-parents/.

Bogotch, I. E. (2000). *Educational leadership and social justice: Theory into practice.* Revised version of paper presented at the annual conference of the University Council for Educational Administration, Albuquerque, NM. ERIC document no. ED 452 585.

Brackenridgs, K. (2020). To overcome the stress of this pandemic, educators must lead with relationships, routines, and resilience. *EdSource.* https://edsource.org/2020/to-overcome-the-stress-of-this-pandemic-educators-must-lead-with-relationships-routines-and-resilience/637163.

Brown, K., and Shaked, H. (2018). *Preparing future leaders for social justice: Bridging theory and practice through a transformative andragogy* (second edition). Rowman and Littlefield.

Catalyst. (2020). The impact of COVID-19 on working parents. https://www.catalyst.org/research/impact-covid-working-parents/.

Cronin, D. (2020, July 13). New study reveals racial disparities among food insecure families. *Harvest Public Media.* https://www.harvestpublicmedia.org/post/new-study-reveals-racial-disparities-among-food-insecure-families.

Eama, A. (2020). I don't trust what the department of education is saying: Parents of color choose all remote learning at higher rates. *GothamGazette* https://www.gothamgazette.com/city/9802-parents-students-of-color-remote-learning-higher-rates-new-york-city-schools-covid.

Farber, Garcia, E., and Weiss, E. (2020). Covid-19 and student performance, equity, and U.S. education policy. Lessons from pre-pandemic research to inform relief, recovery, and rebuilding. *Economic Policy Institute*, 1–60. https://files.epi.org/pdf/205622.pdf.

Garcia, E., and Weiss, E. (2020). COVID-19 and student performance, equity, and U.S. education policy. https://www.epi.org/publication/the-consequences-of-the-covid-19-pandemic-for-education-performance-and-equity-in-the-united-states-what-can-we-learn-from-pre-pandemic-research-to-inform-relief-recovery-and-rebuilding/.

Gershon, M. (2012). Teacher leadership: Leading for social justice in teacher education. In C. Boske and S. Diem (Eds.), *Global leadership for social justice: Taking it from the field to practice* (Advances in Educational Administration, Vol. 14). Emerald Group Publishing. https://doi.org/10.1108/S1479-3660(2012)0000014012.

Gonzáles, K., and Frumkin, R. (2018). *Communicating effectively and meaningfully with diverse families: An action oriented approach for early childhood educators.* Brill-Sense Publishing.

Hackman, H. (2005). Five essential components for social justice education, *Equity and Excellence in Education, 38*(2), 103–9. http://ci563sum09.pbworks.com/f/HACKMAN.PDF.

Hammond, Z. L. (2014). *Culturally responsive teaching and the brain: Promoting authentic engagement and rigor among culturally and linguistically diverse students.* Corwin.

Harris, A., and Jones, M. (2020). COVID 19—school leadership in disruptive times. *School Leadership and Management, 40*(4), 243–47. https://doi.org/10.1080/13632434.2020.1811479.

Kozol, J. (2012). *Savage inequalities: Children in America's schools.* Random House.

Kuhfeld, M., James, S., Tarasawa, B., Johnson, A., Ruzek, E., and Liu, J. (2020). *Projecting the potential impacts of COVID-19 school closures on academic achievement.* (Ed Working Paper: 20–226). Annenberg Institute at Brown University. https://doi.org/10.26300/cdrv-yw05.

Longmuir, F. (2020, July 27). A crisis necessitates change: COVID has laid bare the invisible work for teachers. *Education HQ News.* https://educationhq.com/news/a-crisis-necessitates-change-covid-has-laid-bare-the-invisible-work-of-teachers-79741/.

Martell, M. (2020). *A framework schools can use to make better decisions.* School Leadership. https://www.edutopia.org/article/framework-schools-can-use-make-better-decisions.

Mundoff, J., Beckett, B., Boehm, S., Flake, C., and Miller, C. (2019). From the voices of teachers: Envisioning social justice teacher leadership through portraits of practice. *International Journal of Teacher Leadership, 10*(2), 67–81. https://eric.ed.gov/?id=EJ1244926.

Noguera, P. (2020). Pedro Noguera's Panel on Coronavirus Pandemic and K12 Education Funding. Albert Shanker Institute. https://www.youtube.com/watch?v=SPhTn774fTI.

Oakes, J. (2005). *Keeping track: How schools structure inequality.* Yale University Press.

Rapp, D. (2002). Social justice and the importance of rebellious, oppositional imaginations. *Journal of School Leadership, 12*(3): 226–45. https://doi.org/10.1177/105268460201200301.

Rosenthal, R., and Jacobson, L. (1968). *Pygmalion in the classroom: Teacher expectation and pupils' intellectual development.* Holt, Rinehart and Winston.

Russell, B., Hutchison, M., Tambling, R., Tomkunas, A. J., and Horton, A.L. (2020). Initial challenges of caregiving during Covid-19: Caregiver burden, mental health, and the parent-child relationship. *Child Psychiatry and Human Development, 51,* 671–82. https://link.springer.com/article/10.1007%2Fs10578-020-01037-x.

Saavedra, A., Rapaport, A., Silver, D., Polikoff, M., Garland, M., and Haderlein, S. (2020, August 3). *Parent's perspectives on the effects of COVID-19 on K-12 education, April-July.* USC Schaeffer. https://healthpolicy.usc.edu/evidence-base/parents-perspectives-on-the-effects-of-covid-19-on-k-12-education-april-july-2020/.

Sadker, M., and Sadker, D. (1994). *Failing at fairness: How our schools cheat girls.* Simon and Schuster.

Schleicher, A. (2020). The impact of COVID-19 on education: Insights from education at a glance 2020. https://www.oecd.org/education/the-impact-of-covid-19-on-education-insights-education-at-a-glance-2020.pdf.

Spillane, J. (2005) Distributed leadership. *The Educational Forum, 69*(2), 143–50. https://doi.org/10.1080/00131720508984678.

Spinelli, M, Lionetti, F, Pastore, M., and Fasolo M. (2020). Parents' stress and children's psychological problems in families facing the COVID-19 outbreak in Italy. *Front. Psychol, 11*(1713). https://www.frontiersin.org/articles/10.3389/fpsyg.2020.01713/full.

Spring, J. (2019). *American education: Sociocultural, political, and historical studies in education* (nineteenth edition). Routledge.

Strober, M. M., and Tyack, D. B. (1980). Why do women teach and men manage? *Signs: Journal of Women in Culture and Society, 5*(3), 494–503.

Vegas, E., and Whintrop, R. (2020). Beyond reopening schools: How education can emerge stronger than before COVID-19. https://www.brookings.edu/research/beyond-reopening-schools-how-education-can-emerge-stronger-than-before-covid-19/.

Xiang, M., Zhang, Z., and Kuwahara, K. (2020). Impact of COVID-19 pandemic on children and adolescents' lifestyle behavior larger than expected. *Progress in cardiovascular diseases, 63*(4), 531–32. https://doi.org/10.1016/j.pcad.2020.04.013.

Chapter Ten

Ethical Leadership in Times of Crises
Practical Guidelines and Suggestions
Jeffrey Glanz

PRE-FOCUS GUIDING QUESTIONS

- What are some ethical challenges that principals and other leaders might face in a crisis?
- How would you, as a school leader, create and sustain an ethical organization?
- Do you have a set approach or model from which to confront, analyze, and solve an ethical dilemma? Explain.
- What principles would guide you when you have to make a tough decision that has serious ethical implications?

INTRODUCTION

In the words of Elaine Wilmore (2013), "being a leader is not an easy job" (p. 90). Principals and other school leaders are confronted with ethical and moral dilemmas that are challenging in normal times. In times of crisis, they are exacerbated, as emphasized in chapter 3 when Orly Shapira-Lishchinsky addressed inequity issues that educators must confront and the use of mentoring to empower teachers in grappling with very serious issues affecting students, teachers, and parents. Her discussion was reinforced and extended in chapter 9 by Katia Gonzáles in her discussion of issues of social justice when assessing the impact of a crisis like COVID-19 on students, families, and educators.

Previous research has indicated that educators do not always consider the ethical implications of their work in schools. It is, they say, often assumed or taken for granted (see, e.g., Campbell, 1997; Starratt, 2003). Ethics is viewed, at best, as a subterranean consideration, but not practically relevant as a source of authority (Sergiovanni, 1992) or as a decision-making factor (Shapiro and Stefkovich, 2019). Past research also indicated that school leaders lacked ethical literacy related to their work in school leadership (see, e.g., Begley and Johanson, 2003; Stohr Isaacson, 2007).

Yet, more recently, the notion that school leaders need to be mindful of their ethical responsibilities has garnered greater attention in the literature (Bass et al., 2018; Crawford, 2017; Ehrich et al., 2015). The overarching issue for us today is the degree to which ethical leadership plays a role in dealing with school crises. Framed as a question, what are the more important ethical concerns faced by leaders during a crisis?

The purpose of this final chapter, then, is to alert readers to the ethical and moral responsibilities of leaders as they confront school-related crises. These ethical issues underlie all the topics discussed in the previous chapters. In highlighting many practical suggestions and guidelines to follow, I will draw upon some of the ideas addressed earlier in this book.

More specifically, I will raise important ethical questions that school leaders must address when a crisis strikes. I will use the COVID-19 pandemic crisis as a framework, but the ideas relate to most other types of crises as well. The questions include:

a. What are the ethical issues that a school leader must address?
b. What are some of the important assumptions that school leaders should attend to regarding ethical leadership?
c. How can a principal, for instance, create and sustain an ethical organization that will serve as the foundation for dealing with crises of all sorts?
d. Is there a model that educators can utilize when attempting to resolve an ethical dilemma that emerges during a crisis?
e. What are some basic ethical principles that can serve to guide the work of educators when making some rather difficult decisions during a crisis?
f. What are the key questions a principal should ask prior to making a decision amid a crisis?
g. What is an ethic-of-care approach to crisis management?

SOME ETHICAL ISSUES TO CONSIDER IN A CRISIS

I culled these ideas from extant literature, personal experiences, and those of my associates, as well as reports online (e.g., Atwal and McSorley, 2020; Mazar, 2020; Skeet, 2020). This list is not comprehensive, nor is it in any order of priority:

a. With limited resources (educational, personnel, technological, and financial), what are the criteria used to determine who receives priority?
b. How do we react and address a situation when an employee, student, parent, or administrator does not comply with, in the case of COVID-19, mask-wearing and other mandated safety measures?
c. How do we respond to unreasonable requests from parents, students, teachers, senior administrators, and policymakers?
d. Am I giving enough attention to students at risk?
e. In thinking about Shmuel Shenhav and Ayal Geffon's chapter 8 and the challenges of suddenly changing teaching paradigms from face-to-face to an online teaching environment, almost exclusively, what are the ethical considerations a school leader is likely to face? What are the ethical challenges in a case where some teachers are philosophically in opposition, for a variety of reasons, to teaching online, or are incapable of transitioning to an online teaching format?
f. How can I respond to issues of student neglect by parents or others?
g. How do I respond when a staff member is less than truthful in making declarations, such as, during a crisis when teachers are needed in school, the teacher takes off using her sick days for personal reasons?
h. How do I negotiate policy directives from the Central Office or Ministry of Education that are not aligned with the beliefs and values of the school or key constituents in the school?
i. In reflecting on a few chapters in this book (especially Helen Hazi's chapter 4 on teacher evaluation, Shazia Rehman Khan's chapter 5 on character education, and Haim Shaked's chapter 6 on instructional leadership), how can a principal maintain a focus by supporting ongoing processes of evaluation, supervision, and character education programs when attention, understandably so, is now directed fully at addressing a nonacademic crisis? What are the ethical implications involved in doing so?
j. Specifically related to the COVID-19 pandemic and policymakers, to what extent are we taking ethical responsibility for potentially damaging many students' emotional, psychological, and educational well-being by depriving them of regular, continuous schooling? (see a most interesting and controversial blog: https://gershondistenfeld.blogspot.com/2020/09/sacrificing-our-children-on-altar-of.html)

Leading with conviction and integrity means making the tough choices even in the face of staunch opposition, personally and socially. We need principals with deep-seated convictions, a strong sense of morals, and an unwavering commitment to doing the right thing. As Komives, Lucas, and McMahon (1998) remind us, "leading with a moral purpose is central to the leadership process" (p. 271).

EIGHT ASSUMPTIONS OF ETHICAL LEADERSHIP

This chapter is guided by eight assumptions of ethical leadership reviewed by Komives, Lucas, and McMahon (1998), citing Lucas and Anello (1995):

a. Ethics is the heart of leadership—leading with integrity.
b. All leadership is value-driven—treating others justly and fairly.
c. The journey to ethical leadership begins with an examination of personal values—reflecting on one's core values. These values serve as moral compasses to guide decisions made about ethical dilemmas.
d. Ethical leadership can be learned in a variety of ways—through personal experience, trial and error, reflection, and so on.
e. Ethical leadership involves a connection between ethical thought and action—it's not necessary to learn many ethical theorists and philosophical works, but rather to engage in reflecting personal values applied to real ethical dilemmas.
f. Character development is an essential ingredient of ethical leadership—"walk the talk."
g. Members at all levels of an organization or community have the opportunity and responsibility to participate in the process of exercising ethical leadership—all members of the school have a responsibility to act ethically and advance the core values of the school.
h. Everything we do teaches—we are role models—our actions speak louder than our words.

CREATING AND SUSTAINING AN ETHICAL ORGANIZATION

Aside from behaving ethically and morally as an individual, a principal must be able to facilitate an ethical organization. Nash (1990) identifies four qualities for creating and sustaining an ethical organization:

a. Critical-thinking skills assist an individual to weigh facts and draw conclusions about a given problem or dilemma. Ethical behavior is fostered through critical thinking. Creating a think tank comprised of individuals who think creatively, out of the proverbial box, is highly recommended. Brainstorming solutions to dilemmas or problems with a team of peers is helpful. Utilizing consensus-building strategies is important.
b. Personal integrity means standing up against opposing forces that go against personal or professional ethics. Some principals are conservative and fearful to confront controversial issues. They should reexamine their beliefs and values and ask, "Will I do almost anything to remain true to them?"

c. Looking at situations in a multidimensional way by seeing things from a variety of perspectives is a crucial mindset. By conditioning ourselves to think and see globally, we are better able to understand different ways of solving problems. Examining an educational problem sociologically, legally, psychologically, culturally, philosophically, economically, and politically provides a broad understanding from which to generate possible solutions.
d. Personal motivation to do the right thing is critical. Leadership is about doing the right things, not just doing things right. Affirming one's commitment daily to doing the right thing by asking, "Am I doing the right thing in this situation?" is paramount.

UTILIZING THE REST MODEL TO SOLVE ETHICAL DILEMMAS

Komives, Lucas, and McMahon (1998) relate James Rests's (1986) practical decision-making model that provides four aspects of a decision-making model and is based on "moral reasoning and an ethic of care" (p. 265). The Rest model attempts to help understand and predict moral behavior and decision-making. According to Rest, a student of Lawrence Kohlberg, people go through four stages or components when making a decision about an ethical dilemma: sensitivity, judgment, motivation, and courage. Failing in any one component may mean that a poor decision is likely to be made.

The Rest's Four-Component Decision-Making Model, drawn from Komives, Lucas, and McMahon (1998, p. 266) is outlined below:

Component 1: Moral Sensitivity (interpreting the situation as moral)

A. Being aware of the situation's moral dimension, that is, that the welfare of another person is at stake
B. Recognizing how possible courses of action affect all parties involved

Component II: Moral Judgment (defining the morally ideal course of action)

A. Determining what should be done
B. Formulating a plan of action that applies a moral standard or ideal (e.g., justice)

Component III: Moral Motivation (deciding what to do)

A. Evaluating the various courses of action for how they would serve moral or nonmoral values (e.g., political sensitivity, professional aspirations)
B. Deciding what to do

Component IV: Moral Action (executing and implementing a moral plan of action)

A. Acting as one intended to act; following through with that decision
B. Being assisted by perseverance, resoluteness, strong character, core values, the strength of one's convictions, and so on

APPLYING THE REST MODEL

A moral dilemma a school leader may face during a crisis: A principal is personally very close friends with one of the teachers in his school. Based on recently issued school-board guidelines, it is now the official school policy that all teachers teach within a plastic encasing and that they wear a mask at all times when they are teaching. It has been reported to this principal that his friend, the teacher, has repeatedly violated this school-board ruling. The principal had previously enforced the ruling with another teacher, reprimanding her and giving her a warning to follow the mandated procedure, even though it is difficult to follow. What should this principal do about his friend?

Using the Rest model based on *Component I*, the principal realizes that this case is indeed an ethical issue and not something he can simply "draw under the rug." He understands the nature of the violation and that at least one other teacher has been reprimanded. He also realizes that his decision will likely have consequences for staff morale and so on. Should the principal attempt to ignore the matter? Should he simply, off the record, speak with his friend privately? Should he publically call him to task? Is it fair to even penalize any teacher in the school for a policy that almost everyone in the school agrees is ludicrous and unfair?

Under *Component II*, the principal pauses and considers the morally ideal situation. What would he do if the teacher was not his close friend? How did this principal act in the past about upholding this policy? Should the principal consider the situation a matter of justice and equity, that is, treating all people fairly in similar situations?

Under *Component III*, the principal will have to decide what to do. Using the Rest model, he will consider the impact of his decision on other teachers in his school, on the school board should they discover he has not enforced their mandate, and even on the students, who realize some teachers are adhering to the policy, while others are not. He also considers the impact his decision will have on the ethical climate of his school.

In *Component IV*, he considers the question, among others, "What would he do if the information became public knowledge that he had allowed his friend to 'slide,' so to speak, in this case?" How will this decision affect his future decisions and credibility as an ethical school leader?

ATTENDING TO FIVE PRINCIPLES OF ETHICS

Komives, Lucas, and McMahon (1998) also explain five principles of ethics that provide school leaders a grounding in ethical leadership: 1) respecting autonomy, 2) doing no harm, 3) benefiting others, 4) being just, and 5) being faithful. A principal, can "use these five principles as a critical evaluative approach to moral reasoning and ethical decision-making" (p. 267).

1. *Respecting Autonomy* refers to providing leaders with the freedom of choice, allowing individuals to freely develop their values, and respecting the right of others to act independently. Autonomy, like constitutional rights and liberties, has conditions and does not imply unrestricted freedom. A major assumption of autonomy is that an individual possesses a certain level of competence to make rational and informed decisions.
2. *Doing No Harm (Non-maleficence)* refers to establishing an environment that is free from harm to others, both psychologically and physically. Leaders refrain from actions that can harm others.
3. *Benefiting Others (Beneficence)* refers to promoting the interests of the organization above personal interests and self-gain. The notion of promoting what is good for the whole of the organization or community and promoting the growth of the group is upheld in the principle of beneficence.
4. *Being Just (Justice)* is treating people fairly and equitably. This principle is traced to Aristotle's work on ethics (also see Rawls's 1971 classic work).
5. *Being Faithful (Fidelity)* means keeping promises, being faithful, and being loyal to the group or organization. Being faithful is a principle premised on relationships and trust. If a member of the school violates the principle of fidelity, it is difficult or impossible for others to develop a trusting relationship with that person (Komives et al., 1998, p. 268).

RAISING TWELVE QUESTIONS WHEN MAKING A DECISION

Komives, Lucas, and McMahon (1998) cite Nash (1987), who presents another model for addressing ethical dilemmas. He poses twelve questions leaders should pose before making a decision or take any action related to the ethical problem at hand.

1. Have you defined the problem accurately?
2. How would you define the problem if you stood on the other side of the fence?
3. How did this situation occur in the first place?

4. To whom and to what do you give your loyalty as a person and as a member of the organization?
5. What is your intention in making this decision?
6. How does this intention compare with the probable results?
7. Whom could your decision or action injure?
8. Can you discuss the problem with the affected parties before you make your decision?
9. Are you confident that your position will be as valid over a long period of time as it seems now?
10. Could you disclose without qualm your decision or action to your boss, the president of the board of directors, your family, and society as a whole?
11. What is the symbolic potential of your action if understood? If misunderstood?
12. Under what conditions would you allow exceptions to your stand? (p. 270)

These ethical decision-making principles or models alone will not necessarily help leaders to resolve every dilemma they encounter. They do provide, however, a framework to guide decision-making ethically.

CONCLUSION: THE MORAL IMPERATIVE OF SCHOOL LEADERSHIP IN TIMES OF CRISIS

In times of crisis, the most important disposition that a school leader should possess is that of caring (Kennedy, 2020). Caring for students, parents, teachers, and the community is an axiomatic moral imperative. Nel Noddings, perhaps more than anyone else, framed school leadership on a paradigm of "leadership as an ethic of caring" (1984, 1992).

Such a conception supports the notion that the task of principals is to support and encourage teachers while nurturing children by teaching them to be caring, moral, and productive members of society. Noddings (1992) explains: "The traditional organization of schooling is intellectually and morally inadequate for contemporary society" (p. 173). Nurturing an "ethic of caring," principals, as do teachers, realize their "ultimate motive is to inspire a sense of caring, sensitivity, appreciation, and respect for human dignity of all people despite travails that pervade our society and world" (p. xiv).

Unlike traditional humanistic models of administration, "caring" is inclusionary, nonmanipulative, and empowering. Whereas the main objective of bureaucracy is standardization, caring inspires individual responsibility. Starratt (1993) provides support for an ethic of caring in educational administration. According to Starratt, an administrator committed to an ethic of caring will "be grounded in the belief that the integrity of human relationships should be held sacred and that the school as an organization should hold the good of human beings within it as sacred" (p. 195).

How do principals demonstrate caring and empathy, especially in times of crisis? They: (1) listen to the other's perspective, (2) respond appropriately to the awareness that comes from this reception, and (3) remain committed to others and to the relationship. A principal operating from an "ethic of caring" puts people first and policy second.

Although an ethic of caring is an important paradigm in normal school situations, it takes on heightened significance in times of crisis. During a crisis when tensions run high, a school leader committed to an ethic of caring should not make decisions based on political expediency or arbitrary favoritism. Rather, decisions should be grounded on a care-based concern for all crisis-affected people (Branicki, 2020; Linsley and Slack, 2013). Educational leaders, of all types in all situations, must affirm and continually reaffirm their commitment to moral and ethical integrity.

POST-NOTE

- Can you think of an instance when your values or ethics came into conflict with school or district policy? Explain how you resolved the dilemma.
- Karolyn Snyder and Kristen Snyder in chapter 1 discuss "a new mindset for the continuous improvement and transformation of schooling" in which "digital living, working, and learning will become the new norm for K-12 schools." What ethical implications are embedded in such a move?
- There is recent literature on the idea of an "ethic of caring." Research some of this literature and discuss how an "ethic of caring" can influence your ethical decision-making.
- Lisa Vinnicombe in chapter 2 discusses several challenges that leaders face after a major crisis like COVID-19 hits. Consider the challenges she enumerates and the implications for ethically dealing with them.
- Mary Lynne Derrington and Sonya Hayes in chapter 7 address several different forms of leadership. How does the notion of an "ethic of caring" relate to these various forms of leadership?

REFERENCES

Atwal, K., and McSorley, E. (2020). School leadership during COVID-19: Perspectives from the front line. https://www.birmingham.ac.uk/schools/education/ela/events/2020/school-leadership-during-covid-19.aspx.

Bass, L., Frick, W. C., and Young, M. C. (Eds.). (2018). *Developing ethical principles for school leadership.* Routledge.

Begley, P. T., and Johanson, O. (2003). *The ethical dimensions of school leadership.* Springer.

Branicki, L. J. (2020). COVID-19, ethics of care and feminist crisis management. https://doi.org/10.1111/gwao.12491.

Campbell, E. (1997). Ethical school leadership: Problems of an elusive role. *Journal of School Leadership, 7*(3), 287–300. https://doi.org/10.1177/105268469700700304.

Crawford, E. R. (2017). The ethic of community and incorporating undocumented immigrant concerns into ethical school leadership. *Educational Administration Quarterly, 53*(2), 147–79. https://doi.org/10.1177/0013161X16687005.

Ehrich, L. C., Harris, J., Klenowski, V., Smeed, J., and Spina, N. (2015). The centrality of ethical leadership. *Journal of Educational Administration, 53*(2), 97–214. https://doi.org/10.1108/JEA-10-2013-0110.

Kennedy, K. (2020). Centering equity and caring in leadership for social-emotional learning: Toward a conceptual framework for diverse learners. *Journal of School Leadership, 29*(6), 473–92. https://doi.org/10.1177/1052684619867469.

Komives, S. R., Lucas, N., and McMahon, T. R. (1998). *Exploring leadership.* Jossey-Bass.

Linsley, P. M., and Slack, R. (2013). Crisis management and an ethic of care. *Journal of Business Ethics, 113*(2), 285–95. https://www.jstor.org/stable/23433699.

Lucas, N., and Anello, E. (1995, November). *Ethics and leadership.* Unpublished paper. Salzburg Leadership Seminar. Salzburg, Austria.

Mazar, N. (2020). Ethical leadership at the heart of the COVID-19 crisis. https://www.bu.edu/susilo/2020/04/11/ethical-leadership-at-the-heart-of-the-covid-19-crisis/.

Nash, L. L. (November, 1987). 12 questions to ask when making ethical decisions. *Training and Development Magazine, 36.*

Nash, L. L. (1990). *Good intentions aside.* Harvard Business School Press.

Noddings, N. (1984). *Caring: A feminist approach to ethics and moral education.* University of California Press.

Noddings, N. (1992). *The challenge to care in schools: An alternative approach to education.* Teachers College Press.

Rawls, J. (1971). *A theory of justice.* Oxford University Press.

Rest, J. R. (1986). Moral development in young adults. In R. A. Mines and K. S. Kitchener (Eds.), *Adult cognitive development: Methods and models* (pp. 92–111). Praeger.

Sergiovanni, T. J. (1992). *Moral leadership: Getting to the heart of school improvement.* Jossey-Bass.

Shapiro, J. P., and Stefkovich, J. A. (2019). *Ethical leadership and decision making in education: Applying theoretical perspectives to complex dilemmas.* Routledge.

Skeet, A. (2020). Educational leadership practices in a pandemic. https://www.scu.edu/ethics/leadership-ethics-blog/ethical-leadership-practices-in-a-pandemic/.

Starratt, R. J. (1993). *The drama of leadership.* Falmer Press.

Starratt, R. J. (2003). A perspective on ethical educational leadership: An ethics of presence. In F. C. Lunenburg and C. S. Carr (Eds.), *Shaping the future: Policy, partnerships and emerging perspectives.* ScarecrowEducation.

Stohr Isaacson, L. (2007). *The principal's purpose: A practical guide to moral and ethical school leadership.* Eye on Education.

Wilmore, E. L. (2013). *Principal leadership.* Sage.

Future Directions

It is axiomatic that school leaders must be prepared to deal with crises that inevitably arise. There are, of course, different degrees of crises. For a crisis to arise daily is not unusual, such as confronting an irate parent, a flood in the school's basement, teacher dissatisfaction, and so on. The crises we have discussed in this volume are of a larger magnitude. Regardless of the severity of the situation, an effective school leader must possess several characteristics and skills, including, among others, intestinal fortitude, foresight and insight, a positive long-term outlook, and organizational and interpersonal competencies.

I believe that one of the more important dispositions for any leader, however, is to realize a fundamental premise underlying any crisis. For this idea, I look toward the Chinese character that represents the word "crisis." It is made up of two symbols that convey two ideas: one, danger, and two, opportunity. The message is clear, that is, in any crisis we face we should realize that although danger looms it is an opportunity for growth.

A perusal of the chapters in this book indicates that our authors, regardless of the main subject they addressed, have an abiding belief in our ability and resiliency to effectively confront crises. I would like, in closing, to proffer a few practical, futuristic (innovative) suggestions for preparing school leaders to effectively confront crisis and to offer just a few additional ideas for practicing school leaders.

1. Principal preparation programs should develop either a full course on crisis leadership or include the topic as a major discussion in some relevant other courses, such as Topics in Leadership, Introduction to Leadership, Managerial Leadership, and so on. I conducted an informal online survey of course offerings in educational administration or leadership,

internationally, and found very few programs that have a separate course devoted to crisis leadership or management. Although I didn't check, I presume the topic is discussed somewhat in other courses. Still, especially after the current pandemic, perhaps programs will consider creating a new course devoted to the subject exclusively. We in education at times are reactive rather than proactive. But, I say, better late than never.

2. In a similar vein, preparation programs should focus on problem-based learning. For instance, case studies such as those published by the *Journal of Case Studies* or the *International Journal of Case Studies*, among other journals, should be vigorously incorporated in curricula among programs that prepare school leaders. Such case studies could be part of courses on crisis leadership or even in a course on organizational management.

   My read of the chapters in this volume tells me that dealing with crises can be an overwhelming experience that many school leaders may not be adequately prepared to handle, especially if not addressed in their preparation programs. Therefore, greater attention to incorporating case studies in which candidates are challenged by the realities of various types of crises seems to be in order so that they feel confident to successfully manage them.

3. Another related suggestion is to utilize the field-experience component in preparation programs to challenge candidates in varied ways to grapple with issues related to dealing with a crisis. Although the scope and amount of time devoted to meaningful fieldwork vary across programs internationally, the subject of managing crises should be part of every fieldwork experience. Students could interview practicing school leaders on the subject. They could experience some "mock crises" with the guidance of a mentor and have their peers and the mentor critique their response. Roleplaying is another viable option. Teams or groups of principal candidates could watch videos of real crises in schools and then converse on ways of effectively dealing with them. The possibilities are many. However, the curriculum must be designed to allow for such experiences.

4. [*Note*: The authors in this volume proffered several practical and theoretical strategies for school leaders in handling crises. I am not going to summarize them. Rather, I will add some of my ideas on the subject based on my years of experience in the field as an experienced public school administrator and professor of educational leadership. Some of these ideas may have been mentioned by the authors, but perhaps not in the way I will relate them. I will elucidate just two ideas.]

First, an important rule for preparing to manage a crisis is to "expect the unexpected." Implied in this common-sense admonition is the notion that one must realize that school leadership is a slippery, unpredictable responsibility. This reminds me of a story.

There was once a fellow who worked in an office in some metropolitan city and would leave the building for lunch at noon each day. He would pass the pretzel stand on the corner and place a quarter on the cart but would never take a pretzel. This continued every day, week after week. Finally, the elderly woman running the stand spoke up as the fellow put his daily quarter down without, of course, taking a pretzel. "Sir, may I have a word with you?" she asked. The fellow said, "I know what you're going to say. You're going to ask me why I give you a quarter every day and don't take a pretzel." The woman responded, "Not at all, I just wanted to tell you that the price is now 35 cents!"

Learning to expect the unexpected when serving in a leadership capacity, especially in schools, is a required mindset that goes a long way to preventing being taken off guard when a crisis of any sort develops. Leading is not a neat, uncomplicated process of applying "four easy steps." Successful leaders often *expect* certain situations to occur. Experienced principals will tell you that if a day passes by without something unusual happening then that itself is unusual.

When some crisis emerges, either suddenly or slowly over time, an effective principal is prepared. Of course, we cannot foresee everything that may happen, but once we are aware that endless possibilities exist, we're less likely to be surprised and caught off guard.

Each crisis has its unique circumstances. Overall, however, a school leader should be prepared to react. Despite the preparation one may, hopefully, receive in one's master's degree program in educational leadership, one reacts, most naturally, based on one's personality. Some people are naturally calm, while others are slightly hyper. I do not think one way of reacting is necessarily superior to the other. I have seen "laid-back" leaders muffle a crisis, and I have also seen an anxious leader overact inappropriately. One must utilize one's natural dispositions and channel them positively. This can only occur when one is prepared to meet a crisis, as emphasized in the first three suggestions above.

Second, a school leader is expected to take concerted action in a crisis. Allow me first to relate the story and then I will explicate its message.

There is a story about a geologist who was researching in Alaska in 1964. That also happened to be the year a great earthquake hit. It seems that the geologist was at home when he felt the floor suddenly sway under him. Then the walls buckled, and finally part of the roof collapsed. With the earthquake in full tilt, so to speak, Joe ran outside to see a street full of people shocked, confused, and helpless. At that point, his neighbor, with a child under each arm, rushed up to him and said, "Joe, you're a geologist! For God's sake, do something!"

Like the geologist in the story, we, as educational leaders, are also asked to respond to problems and crises and to "do something." To take thoughtful, yet decisive action to meet the challenges we face is our greatest task. However, we must do so with deliberation. Leaders need to be prepared strategically. Allow me to share one simple plan that includes a series of steps, explained briefly, that leaders may find helpful regardless of the nature of the crisis. As I said above, dealing with crises is not a simple step-by-step process, yet some simple general guidelines are valuable.

Step 1: When a crisis occurs, step back, deliberate, and define the crisis (its nature, scope, and related factors). Doing so with one's leadership team is suggested, because the coalition of minds on the current crisis will help to clarify the exigencies of the moment to make more effective decisions (short- and long-term).

Step 2: Consider all the various constituencies that are affected by the crisis. Simultaneously, consider the educational, social, cultural, political, economic, and interpersonal implications for each constituent of any decisions that are made.

Step 3: Share ideas with the team about various resources (e.g., financial, personnel, specialists, etc.) that should be available to address the crisis. For example, as regards the COVID-19 pandemic, technology specialists were very much needed to provide professional development (PD) and support to teachers who had never taught an online course in the past.

Step 4: Take action and assess its impact, positive or, perhaps, not so positive. If the latter, then the team reconvenes to discuss additional strategies to deal with the crisis in its various facets. The key idea here is to think-implement-monitor-reassess.

Step 5: Returning to a sense of normalcy after a crisis passes is not as easy as it may appear. The impact of the crisis might have lingering effects. Thoughtful leaders remain cognizant of these effects and are ready to take appropriate action to provide needed assistance.

Crisis and Pandemic Leadership used the COVID-19 pandemic as a frame or vantage point, given its currency at the time of publication, to discuss various issues that can relate to any school crisis. Although much more can be written on this subject, it is my hope as the editor that we have raised for our readers a variety of relevant topics for consideration.

I hope readers will contact our contributors to continue the conversation about these crucial topics. I know, as the editor, I would enjoy readers contacting me to offer suggestions for future topics that might be equally, if not more important to consider. As I mentioned in the Series Editor Introduction, I would be pleased to consider proposals for books on this topic or any other relevant topic for educational leaders.

I wish you all continued success in your important work.

Jeffrey Glanz
March 2021

Index

Australian Institute of School Leadership (AITSL), 25–26

Bronfenbrenner, 38–39; socio-ecological model (SEM), 38, 39, 41

chaos theory, 11–13
character education, 59; aims of, 59–60; challenges of, 60; and Dewey, 62–63; ethics of recognition, 64; goals of, 60–61; and Honneth, 63; rethinking, 61–63; self-reflection, 66; values 15, 19, 25, 61, 67, 77, 128, 130, 133; virtue-based, 61
Corbett Preparatory School (CPS), 13–19
COVID-19 pandemic, 5, 7, 12, 14–16, 19, 23, 25, 30, 35, 38, 48, 63, 84, 101, 104, 113–14, 126, 140; affects, 35–36; Australian context, 24–27; challenges, 36; future directions, 137–41; lockdowns, 28; pervasiveness, 7; post-crisis, 24, 29–30; responses, 49–50, 140

energy system, 8, 10, 12; energy and connections, 9, 121
equitable, 39, 113

families and students, 42, 90–91, 95–96, 113–15; communication, 91; connectivity, 91–92, 95–96; impact of crisis on, 7–8, 118–19; inequity, 25–28, 35, 37–39, 90; social justice for, 115–18
field of educational leadership, 1, 4; research questions, 1–3
Flipboard, 65

goals of schooling, 7, 8, 71, 74–75, 78

instructional leadership:
and goals of schooling, 74–75; core area, 72–73; differentiated, 103; dimensions of, 72; in crisis, 77–79; in practice, 75–77

leadership:
caretaker, 88–89; crisis, 25–26, 35, 83–85, 107–8; crisis guidelines, 25–26; ethical decision-making, 131–32; ethical organization, 128–29; ethics, 125–27, 128; human side of, 23; imperatives of, 24; innovation in, 24; open leadership style, 108; pedagogic, 106; preparedness for, 5; principles of ethics, 131.
See also instructional leadership

learning:
  autonomous, 103, 106; blended learning, 16; cooperative learning, 15, 17–18; faith in students' ability, 106; hybrid learning, 17; models of, 28; self-motivation, 103; servant, 87–88; shared, 15–17; student-autonomy, 103.
  See also teacher mentoring; teaching and pedagogy

National Preparedness Leadership Initiative (NPLI), 83–85

Organization for Economic Cooperation and Development (OECD), 8

principal:
  as instructional leader, 28–29, 50–51, 67; leadership, 14–16, 19, 83; meta-leader, 85–87; personal attributes, 85–86; suggestions for, 43, 119–21, 140
Program for International Student Assessment (PISA), 8
public policy, 38, 39, 42

Rest model, 129–30

schools/schooling:
  challenges of, 5, 8–9, 12, 39, 41–42, 101, 133; complex adaptive systems, 13, 15–18, 20; crises, 5, 9, 31, 35, 38, 40, 47, 59, 60, 64, 71, 83, 85, 97, 101, 105, 113, 126, 137; as living systems, 8–9, 11–13; nature of change, 8–9, 11; pedagogical change, 106, 108; planning, 15–17, 84, 95; sustainability, 9–10, 12, 19–20; systems thinking, 8–9, 12, 13, 1
the sciences:
  big ideas, 8–20; goals of, 71–72; stakeholders, 91, 95–97
self-determination theory, 103

teacher evaluation:
  nature of, 51–52; problems with, 47–48, 52–54
teacher mentoring, 36, 38–41; practical guidelines, 42–43; simulations, 39–42
teaching and pedagogy, 105–7; crisis pedagogy, 102, 104; student-oriented, 104–7
teaching/teachers:
  asynchronous, 104, 105; challenges of, 39–41; collaboration, 15–16, 19; connectivity, 93–94; interdependence, 13, 16, 19; as mentoring, 103; methods of, 101; suggestions for, 43, 119–21; synchronous, 18, 104, 105; team teaching, 15, 17–19; uncertainty of, 23–24, 48–50; well-being and support, 94
technology:
  advocates for, 89; challenges, 90; digital culture, 17–18; distance learning, 104–6; informal, 64–65; online learning, 7, 15, 18, 102–6; online schooling, 59, 64
TPACK model, 104
twenty-first-century skills, 8, 102–4

VUCA model, 104, 107–8

World Economic Forum, 7–8

About the Editor and Contributors

Jeffrey Glanz, EdD, is professor and head of the MEd program in leadership and management in educational Systems at Michlalah Jerusalem College. He held the Silverstein Endowed Chair in Professional Ethics and Values and was a tenured professor of education and administration at the Azrieli Graduate School of Yeshiva University. He was dean of graduate studies and chair of education at Wagner College in Staten Island, New York. He was executive assistant to the president at Kean University and at Kean was named Graduate Teacher of the Year by the Student Graduate Association. He was also the recipient of the Presidential Award for Outstanding Scholarship. He was a teacher and school administrator in New York City for twenty years. Professor Glanz has authored, coauthored, edited, and coedited twenty-two books on various educational topics, including three books with Rowman & Littlefield Publishers: 1) *Revisiting Dewey: Best Practices for Educating the Whole Child Today* (2010, coauthored with Daniel Stuckart); 2) *Action Research: An Educational Leader's Guide to School Improvement* (2014, author); and 3) *Supervision: New Perspectives in Theory and Practice* (2015, coedited with Sally Zepeda). He can be reached at yosglanz@gmail.com or at www.jeffreyglanz.com.

* * *

Mary Lynne Derrington, EdD, is associate professor in educational leadership and policy studies at the University of Tennessee. Her research interests include teacher evaluation, qualitative longitudinal methods, policy implementation, and aspiring female superintendents. Following her research expertise, Dr. Derrington has published refereed articles, book chapters, and books on these topics. She coordinates the doctor of education program and teaches courses in leadership and policy. She can be reached at mderring@utk.edu.

Ayal Geffon is lecturer at Michlalah Jerusalem College in Bayit Vegan, Jerusalem, Israel, and a doctoral student at the Hebrew University, Jerusalem. His dissertation explores the dialectic between teacher authority and student autonomy. His ethnographic research uses the case of higher Jewish (yeshiva) education in order to understand the nature of authority in an environment that encourages student autonomy. He analyzes student interactions with different forms of authority. He has published in journals such as the *International Journal of Educational Reform*. He can be reached at aygeffon@gmail.com.

Katia Gonzáles, EdD, received her doctorate from Columbia University, Teachers College in New York. Dr. Gonzáles is professor and chair of education at Wagner College in New York. Dr. Gonzáles's expertise is in early childhood special education, curriculum development, and culturally responsive practices in teacher education. Her research interests include the role of intercultural communication and culturally responsive practices in early childhood, strategies and techniques to enhance and measure critical thinking, and the impact of community and family in inclusive education. She can be reached at katia.gonzalez@wagner.edu.

Sonya Hayes, PhD, is an assistant professor in the Department of Educational Leadership and Policy Studies at the University of Tennessee. Her research interests include leadership development and support for both pre- and post-service school principals, principal preparation, and leadership for learning. Specifically, she is interested in how principals are prepared and supported for the complex and demanding role of improving teaching and learning through mentoring and coaching paradigms. Dr. Hayes has published her research in numerous journals and book chapters. She can be reached at shayes22@utk.edu.

Helen M. Hazi, PhD, is professor emerita of educational leadership at West Virginia University and was a teacher, a supervisor of curriculum and instruction, a curriculum specialist, and an expert witness. She is the founder of the Supervision and Instructional Leadership AERA-SIG. Dr. Hazi writes about legal issues that have a consequence for the discourse communities of supervision in books and journals such as the *Journal of Educational Supervision*, *Journal of Staff Development*, and *Educational Policy Analysis Archives*. Recent topics include teacher evaluation instruments, statutes, litigation and marketing; professional development; and instructional improvement. She can be reached at hmhazi@verizon.net or https://helenhazi.faculty.wvu.edu.

Shazia Rehman Khan, PhD, is assistant professor in the Department of Business Studies. Dr. Khan teaches ethics, character building, and leadership at Bahria University, Islamabad, Pakistan. She has published articles on leadership and ethical decision-making. Her research interests include ethical decision-making, identity formation, leadership, and meaningful work. Her current work revolves around the idea of misrecognition of employees in the organization. She can be reached at shazia.buic@bahria.edu.pk.

Haim Shaked, PhD, is associate professor and president of Hemdat Hadarom College of Education, Sdot Negev, Israel. As a scholar-practitioner with almost twenty years of experience as a school principal, his research focuses on principalship, and in particular on instructional leadership and system thinking in school leadership. On these topics, he has published more than fifty refereed research articles, book chapters, edited books, and authored books. He can be reached at haim.shaked@hemdat.ac.il or https://haimshaked.com/.

Orly Shapira-Lishchinsky, PhD, is full professor and head of the Department of Educational Administration, Leadership and Policy, School of Education, at Bar-Ilan University, Israel. Most recently, she was awarded funding from the European Union's Horizon 2020 Research and Innovation Programme for her project: "Interdisciplinary Models of Schooling: Exploring Ethical Culture in International Science Assessments." She has published two books, sixty articles in international refereed journals, and participated in about fifty international conferences. Some of her research interests include organizational ethics, mentoring through simulations, teachers' withdrawal behaviors, and international assessments in science and math (TIMSS). She can be reached at shapiro4@biu.ac.il or https://ronitoved1.wixsite.com/mysite.

Shmuel Shenhav, PhD, is head of the Graduate School of Education at Michlalah Jerusalem College, in Bayit Vegan, Jerusalem, Israel, Head of the Avney Rosha Program for the training of school leaders in the Israel Ministry of Education, and Head of the National-Religious Center for Leadership in Israel. He served as a school principal for many years. He is a national speaker on issues related to educational leadership and has published in journals such as the *International Journal of Educational Reform*. He can be reached at shenhav@huji.ac.il.

Karolyn J. Snyder, PhD, for over fifty years, has served education as a teacher, school leader, professor, and president of the International School Connection, Inc. With over 300 publications and professional work in forty countries, her work has been grounded in a Systems Approach to school development, as well as newer developments in physics that offer guidance for leading school change over time. Over the last thirty years, she has also worked with schools and universities around the world to prepare students as competent and caring global citizens. She can be reached at Karolyn@karolynsnyder.com.

Kristen M. Snyder, PhD, is professor in quality management and associate professor in education at Mid Sweden University. Snyder has contributed to school and leadership development internationally through a variety of programs including the International School Connection. She is the author of numerous publications on leadership and innovation in schools, including the coauthored book, *Living on the Edge of Chaos: Leading Schools into the 21st Century*. She has also developed three benchmarking tools for helping leaders foster schools as sustainable quality organizations. She can be reached at kristen@kcreations.se.

Lisa Vinnicombe, PhD, is postdoctoral research fellow at the REDI (Research for Educational Impact) Centre at Deakin University, Melbourne, Australia. She was an assistant principal at a high-performing secondary school in inner-city Melbourne. Her PhD thesis was a case study on teachers who managed mandated pedagogical change in their daily work. Her areas of research interests include teacher and principal health and well-being, teacher professionalism and practice, and school leadership. During the COVID-19 pandemic, she conducted an online teacher study with a range of teachers from schools across Victoria on the impact of remote learning and school closures on teachers' well-being and the degree to which they adapted to teaching online. She can be reached at lisa.vinnicombe@deakin.edu.au.

www.ingramcontent.com/pod-product-compliance
Lightning Source LLC
Chambersburg PA
CBHW030142240426
43672CB00005B/227